UNTRADITIONAL
DESSERTS

UNTRADITIONAL DESSERTS

100 CLASSIC TREATS WITH A TWIST

ALLISON MILLER

FOUNDER OF TORNADOUGH ALLI

PAGE STREET
PUBLISHING CO.

PAGE STREET
PUBLISHING CO.

First published in 2018 by
Page Street Publishing Co.
27 Congress Street, Suite 105
Salem, MA 01970
www.pagestreetpublishing.com

Distributed by Macmillan, sales in Canada by The Canadian Manda Group.

22   21   20   19   18   1   2   3   4   5

ISBN-13: 978-1-62414-625-1
ISBN-10: 1-62414-625-2

Library of Congress Control Number: 2018951646

Cover and book design by Laura Gallant for Page Street Publishing Co.
Photography by Allison Miller

Printed and bound in the United States

DEDICATION

To my kids, thank you for being such motivators and making me strive to be a better version of myself each and every day.

To my husband, for helping me through all of my meltdowns and almost-giving-ups and for pushing me to continue when life gets hard.

To my mom, for taking my late-night ranting phone calls and answering questions and inspiring me to always love what I do.

And to my dad, for being the person who never shied away from trying my crazy made-up concoctions as a kid and now as an adult.

I wouldn't be who I am without all these amazing people in my life, and I wouldn't know what life is without them.

CONTENTS

CAPTIVATING CUPCAKES 131

SWEET BEGINNINGS 159

THIS AND THAT 185

INTRODUCTION

"Baking may be regarded as a science, but it's the chemistry between the ingredients and the cook that gives desserts life. Baking is done out of love, to share with family and friends, to see them smile."

—Anna Olson

My name is Alli and I'm a dessertaholic—if there is such a thing. I enjoy cakes, cookies, pies, bars and everything in between. I wholeheartedly believe in NEVER going to bed without dessert. I live and breathe sugar.

I'm the creator behind Tornadough Alli, a website about fast-fix family favorites, delicious desserts and crazy cakes. I don't ever do anything halfway. I prefer homemade over boxed, but I don't shy away from shortcuts either. Some of the best desserts are semi-homemade.

I'm the wife of Jeremy, or "Mr. Non-Sweets Lover," as I've so dubbed him over the eleven years of our marriage. Although, I have finally convinced him to try everything once, and twice if he likes it. I'm a mom to four amazing, crazy, sweet, smart kids: three boys, Jaiden, Keagen and Avery, and the little "princess," Novalee. Without these little beings in my life, I wouldn't have aspired to accomplish the things I have been able to.

I'm a Midwest girl, hailing from a small Minnesota town where I have been cooking and baking (if that's what you call it) since I was very little. My dad willingly taste tested my random concoctions before I knew what did and didn't go together, and he never shied away from letting me experiment, as that was how I quickly learned exactly what did and didn't work.

My mother, the real baker of the family, handed down some valuable lessons over the years, and I have not taken one of them into consideration. Just kidding, I take them into consideration when I see fit. I'm kind of a rebel in the kitchen like that.

As you can see with *Untraditional Desserts*, these recipes are off the wall, crazy and delicious. There are no limits, no rules and no guidelines to the flavors in this book. This book represents my personality with flavors, taking some of my favorite desserts and giving them new life in new forms.

These recipes will inspire you to get creative. Just because something is one flavor doesn't mean that flavor has to stick with just that treat. Push the limits in the kitchen. Be bold, have fun and take risks.

In this book you will find every flavor under the sun—from banana split (page 89), strawberry shortcake (page 82), strawberry cheesecake (page 172) and snickerdoodle (page 34)—but not in the forms you expect.

Think outside the box with recipes like Churro Cheesecake (page 40), Rocky Road Cupcakes (page 138), Pecan Pie Granola (page 197) and Crème Brûlée French Toast Bake (page 160). You have all your favorite flavors, but in untraditional forms!

This book is fun, inspiring and anything but basic. If I can say anything about this book that will stick with you it is that there is absolutely no "normal" in life. There is no one mold that anything has to fit. Everything is different and fun, and hopefully that inspires you to roll with it, take chances and be yourself!

OUTRAGEOUS

OUT-OF-THE-BOX CAKES

Who can go wrong with a delicious cake? I say nobody. Cake is life to me, and I love all sorts of cakes. Layer cake, cake rolls, sheet cakes or Bundt cakes, I leave no stone unturned. You name it, I love it. This chapter is filled with fun cake twists that make you think outside the box on your favorite cake flavors. Think Shirley Temple (page 17), root beer float (page 32) and orange creamsicle (page 20)!

COCONUT CARAMEL COOKIE BUNDT CAKE

I was never a Girl Scout, but it's hard to pass up those Samoas when they come along. I took one of my favorite flavors and turned it into this Bundt cake. Chocolate and vanilla cake is glazed with a coconut-caramel topping that puts that cookie to shame!

SERVES 12 TO 16

¼ cup (25 g) unsweetened cocoa powder, plus more for dusting the pan

1¼ cups (300 g) unsalted butter, softened

2 cups (400 g) granulated sugar

2 tsp (10 ml) vanilla extract

2 tsp (10 ml) almond extract

5 eggs

¾ cup (180 ml) milk

½ cup (60 g) sour cream

3 cups (360 g) all-purpose flour

2 tsp (7 g) baking powder

1 tsp baking soda

½ tsp salt

⅓ cup (80 ml) hot water

CARAMEL GLAZE

1 (14-oz [397-g]) can sweetened condensed milk

1 (11-oz [308-g]) package caramels or caramel bits

2 cups (150 g) coconut, toasted

Preheat the oven to 350°F (177°C, or gas mark 4). Grease a 10-cup (2-L) Bundt pan with shortening or butter, then sprinkle with some cocoa powder. Set aside.

In a stand mixer, beat together your butter and sugar until fluffy. Add in your vanilla and almond extracts until combined. Add the eggs one at a time, mixing well after each addition.

In a small bowl, whisk together your milk and sour cream. Add it to your butter mixture, beating until combined.

In another bowl, whisk together the flour, baking powder, baking soda and salt. Slowly add it to your wet mixture until incorporated. Pour half of your batter into a large bowl. Set aside.

In a small bowl, whisk together your cocoa powder and hot water, and mix it into the batter that was removed. Spread the chocolate layer into the bottom of the prepared pan, then spoon your vanilla mixture on top of the chocolate layer. Bake in the oven for 1 hour until the center is set.

Remove the cake from the oven, and let it cool for about 5 minutes in the pan before turning it out onto a wire rack placed over a baking sheet to cool completely.

To make the caramel glaze, add your sweetened condensed milk and caramels to a medium-size saucepan. Heat over medium heat until smooth, about 3 to 4 minutes. Immediately pour over your cake, spreading around the top and sides. Sprinkle with your toasted coconut, pressing it up the sides and into the center.

SHIRLEY TEMPLE CAKE

Growing up, Shirley Temples were always my favorite drink. In my eyes, 7Up and cherries were the best flavor combination. This cake really brings that childhood drink to life with citrusy layers filled and frosted with a cherry buttercream. It's the iconic drink—in a cake form!

SERVES 12 TO 16

1½ cups (360 g) unsalted butter, softened

3 cups (600 g) granulated sugar

5 eggs

3 cups (360 g) all-purpose flour

2 tsp (10 ml) lemon extract

¾ cup (180 ml) lemon-lime pop, such as 7Up

FROSTING

2 cups (480 g) unsalted butter, softened

7 cups (700 g) powdered sugar

¾ cup (180 ml) maraschino cherry juice

Maraschino cherries, for garnish

White decorating sugar, for garnish

Preheat the oven to 325°F (163°C, or gas mark 3). Line three 8-inch (20-cm) round cake pans with parchment paper and spray with nonstick cooking spray. Set aside.

In a stand mixer, beat together your butter and sugar until light and fluffy. Add in your eggs, and beat until blended. Add in your flour, and mix again until combined. Lastly, add in your lemon extract and lemon-lime pop until incorporated.

Spread the batter evenly among your 3 pans, and bake for 35 to 40 minutes until the center is set. Remove the cakes from the oven, and let them cool slightly before removing to cool completely on wire racks.

To make the frosting, in a stand mixer, beat your butter until smooth. Add in your powdered sugar 1 cup (100 g) at a time until incorporated. Slowly add in your cherry juice until the desired consistency and flavor are reached.

To assemble the cake, place one of your cake layers onto a turntable or cake round. Remove ¾ cup (184 g) of your frosting and set it aside. Spread ¾ cup (184 g) of frosting onto the layer, then top with the second layer of cake and spread another ¾ cup (184 g) of frosting over the top of that layer. Add the third layer on top, then frost the outside and top of the cake with the remaining frosting.

To decorate, add the frosting you set aside to a piping bag fitted with an open star tip. Pipe swirls over the top of the cake. Place the maraschino cherries on top of each swirl, then sprinkle the top of the cake with decorating sugar.

MONSTER-COOKIE SHEET CAKE

Monster cookies are one of my favorite cookies. They have all the good stuff: oats, chocolate chips, peanut butter and M&Ms. When you take that cookie and turn it into a delicious sheet cake, you get your mind blown away with a rich, moist and tasty treat that is hard to resist.

SERVES 20 TO 24

1½ cups (150 g) old-fashioned oats

2 cups (475 ml) boiling water

¾ cup (180 g) unsalted butter, softened

1 cup (200 g) granulated sugar

1 cup (180 g) brown sugar

3 eggs

2 tsp (10 ml) vanilla extract

2 cups (240 g) all-purpose flour

1½ tsp (7 g) baking soda

1 tsp baking powder

1 tsp salt

FROSTING

1 cup (240 g) unsalted butter, softened

1 cup (180 g) creamy peanut butter

4 cups (400 g) powdered sugar

¼ cup (60 ml) milk

Mini chocolate chips, for garnish

M&Ms, for garnish

Preheat the oven to 350°F (177°C, or gas mark 4). Line a 12 x 17-inch (30 x 43-cm) baking pan with parchment paper and spray with nonstick cooking spray. Set aside.

In a medium bowl, add your oats and pour the boiling water over the top. Set aside to let the oats soak up the moisture.

In a stand mixer, beat together your butter and sugars until light and fluffy. Add in your eggs and vanilla, and continue to beat until mixed. In a separate bowl, whisk together the flour, baking soda, baking powder and salt. Slowly add the dry mixture into the butter mixture until incorporated. Lastly, add in the soaked oats and mix until combined.

Spread the batter into the prepared pan, and bake in the oven for 20 to 25 minutes until golden. Remove the cake from the oven, and set it aside to cool.

To make the frosting, in a stand mixer, beat together your butter and peanut butter until smooth. Add in your powdered sugar 1 cup (100 g) at a time until combined. Mix in your milk, and beat on high for 1 to 2 minutes until fluffy.

Spread the frosting over the cooled cake, and sprinkle the chocolate chips and M&Ms over top.

ORANGE CREAMSICLE CAKE

Who else grew up eating all the creamsicle bars that they could? This flavor has always been one of my favorites! With this easy cake, you have two yellow cakes poked and poured with orange Jell-O, and filled and frosted with a light, flavorful cream cheese frosting.

―――――――――――――――――― SERVES 12 TO 16 ――――――――――――――――――

1 (15.25-oz [432-g]) box yellow cake mix, plus the ingredients called for on the package

1 (3-oz [85-g]) box orange Jell-O®

1 cup (240 ml) boiling water

FROSTING

1 (8-oz [230-g]) package cream cheese, softened

2 cups (200 g) powdered sugar

2 tsp (10 ml) vanilla extract

Zest of 1 orange

2 cups (480 ml) heavy whipping cream

Orange gummy candies, for garnish

Orange sugar sprinkles, for garnish

Bake the cake according to the package directions for 2 (8-inch [20-cm]) cake pans.

When ready, remove the cakes from the oven and let them cool in the pans for 5 minutes before turning them out onto a cooling rack to cool completely. Wash your pans, wrap the insides with plastic wrap, and place the cooled cake layers inside. Using a fork, poke holes all over the tops of the cakes. Set aside.

In a medium bowl, add your orange Jell-O and boiling water, and whisk together until the Jell-O is dissolved. Once dissolved, pour it evenly over your cakes. Cool for about 2 hours to let the Jell-O set.

To make the frosting, in a stand mixer fitted with the paddle attachment, beat your cream cheese until smooth. Add in your powdered sugar, vanilla and orange zest. In another large bowl, add your heavy whipping cream and beat with a hand mixer until stiff peaks form. Fold this mixture into your cream cheese mixture until combined.

To assemble your cake, place one layer of the cake on a cake stand or turntable. Top with 1½ cups (367 g) of your frosting. Top with the remaining cake layer. Frost the tops and sides with the remaining frosting until covered. Garnish with the orange gummy candies and sprinkles. Keep refrigerated.

APPLE SPICE PIECAKEN

Is it a pie? Is it a cake? No, it's a piecaken! A whole apple pie is stuffed and baked inside a flavorful spice cake and glazed with a cinnamon–cream cheese topping. This is a real showstopper of a dessert! It's a great conversation starter and a perfect meal ender.

SERVES 8 TO 10

1 (15.25-oz [432-g]) box spice cake mix

1¼ cups (300 ml) milk

1 cup (240 g) unsalted butter, melted

4 eggs

1 (9-inch [23-cm]) fresh baked apple pie

GLAZE

1 (8-oz [230-g]) package cream cheese, softened

¼ cup (60 g) unsalted butter, softened

1 tsp vanilla extract

1 tsp cinnamon

1½ cups (150 g) powdered sugar

2–4 tbsp (30–60 ml) milk

Preheat the oven to 350°F (177°C, or gas mark 4). Line the bottom of a 10-inch (25-cm) springform pan with parchment paper, and spray with nonstick cooking spray. Set aside.

In a large bowl, mix together your cake mix, milk, butter and eggs, and beat with a hand mixer until smooth. Pour half of your mixture into the bottom of the prepared pan. Turn your pie face down into the pan, and pour the remaining cake mixture over top and spread it out.

Bake in the oven for 1 hour, checking after 30 minutes to see if the edges are browning. If the edges are getting brown after the 30-minute mark, place a sheet of tinfoil over the top. After 60 minutes, use a toothpick to check the center for doneness. Remove the piecaken from the oven, and let it cool.

To make the glaze, beat together the cream cheese and butter with a hand mixer until smooth. Add in the vanilla, cinnamon and powdered sugar until incorporated. Add in your milk 1 tablespoon (15 ml) at a time until you reach your desired pourable consistency. Pour over the cooled piecaken.

HOT CHOCOLATE BUNDT CAKE

My kids are some of the biggest hot chocolate fans ever. So, making a hot chocolate cake was a no-brainer. A delicious chocolate Bundt cake is glazed with a gooey and tasty marshmallow glaze, turning that cold weather drink into a moist and tender dessert.

SERVES 12 TO 16

½ cup (50 g) unsweetened cocoa powder, plus more for dusting the pan

1 cup (240 g) unsalted butter, softened

2 cups (400 g) granulated sugar

2 eggs

1 tbsp (15 ml) vanilla extract

1 cup (120 g) sour cream

2 tsp (10 g) baking soda

2½ cups (300 g) all-purpose flour

½ tsp salt

1 cup (240 ml) hot brewed coffee

GLAZE

1 cup (85 g) marshmallow cream

¼ cup (25 g) powdered sugar

2-3 tbsp (30-45 ml) milk

Preheat the oven to 350°F (177°C, or gas mark 4). Grease a 10-cup (2-L) Bundt pan with shortening or butter, then dust with cocoa powder. Set aside.

In a stand mixer, beat together your butter and sugar until fluffy. Add in your eggs, vanilla and sour cream, and mix until combined.

In another bowl, whisk together your cocoa powder, baking soda, flour and salt. Slowly add your dry ingredients to your wet ingredients until just combined. With a mixer on low, slowly pour in your coffee until well mixed.

Pour the cake batter into the prepared Bundt pan, and bake in the oven for 1 hour until the center is set. When ready, remove the cake from the oven, and let it cool in the pan for 5 minutes before transferring to a wire rack to cool completely.

To make the glaze, in a bowl with a hand mixer, mix together your marshmallow cream and powdered sugar until combined. Add in your milk 1 tablespoon (15 ml) at a time until you reach the desired consistency.

Drizzle the glaze over the cooled cake.

LEMON BAR LAVA CAKES

One thing that I loved more than anything growing up was lemon bars. Who can resist the punch of citrus? I know that it's an addicting flavor that I can't resist. What's even better is that these Lemon Bar Lava Cakes take my longtime favorite and turn it into a molten, single-serving treat. White chocolate and lemon collide to make this ooey, gooey dessert.

MAKES 4

1 (4-oz [113-g]) white chocolate baking bar, chopped

½ cup (120 g) unsalted butter

¾ cup (75 g) powdered sugar

2 eggs

2 egg yolks

1 tbsp (15 ml) lemon juice

2 tsp (4 g) lemon zest

¼ tsp salt

¼ cup (30 g) all-purpose flour

Powdered sugar, for garnish

Preheat the oven to 425°F (218°C, or gas mark 7). Grease 4 (6-oz [180-ml]) ramekins with shortening or butter. Set aside.

In a microwave-safe bowl, melt together your chocolate and butter using the microwave, stirring every 30 seconds until smooth. Stir your powdered sugar, eggs, egg yolks, lemon juice, lemon zest and salt into your melted chocolate until combined, then fold in your flour.

Divide the batter evenly among the ramekins. Bake for 15 to 20 minutes until the top is golden and the center is set but still jiggly. Remove the cakes from the oven and let them cool slightly, then run a knife around the edges of the ramekins to loosen the cakes and invert them onto plates.

Sprinkle with powdered sugar, if desired.

PEANUT BUTTER AND JELLY SHEET CAKE

Want to relive your childhood but in dessert form? This Peanut Butter and Jelly Sheet Cake is a fun twist on a classic PB and J sandwich! You will feel your youth all over again as you devour each and every bite of this moist and flavorful cake.

SERVES 20 TO 24

CAKE

3 cups (380 g) all-purpose flour

1¾ cups (340 g) granulated sugar

1½ tsp (6 g) baking powder

½ tsp salt

4 large eggs

¾ cup (180 ml) vegetable oil

1 cup (240 ml) milk

1½ tbsp (22 ml) vanilla extract

1 (20-oz [567-g]) jar grape jelly

FROSTING

2 cups (465 g) unsalted butter, softened

1 (16-oz [454-g]) container creamy peanut butter

6 cups (600 g) powdered sugar

Chopped peanuts, optional

Preheat the oven to 350°F (177°C, or gas mark 4). Line a 12 x 17–inch (32 x 44–cm) rimmed baking sheet with parchment paper and spray with nonstick cooking spray. Set aside.

In a large bowl, whisk together your flour, sugar, baking powder and salt until blended. Add in your eggs, oil, milk and vanilla, and continue to whisk until smooth.

Pour the batter into the prepared pan. Bake in the oven for 20 to 25 minutes or until it springs back when touched and is slightly golden. Remove the cake from the oven, and set it aside to cool.

While the cake is cooling, add your jelly to a bowl. Stir until the jelly loosens and any clumps are broken up and smooth. Spread it over the cooled cake. Cover and let chill in the refrigerator for about 30 minutes.

To make the frosting, in the bowl of a stand mixer fitted with the paddle attachment, add your softened butter and peanut butter. Beat until smooth, then add in your powdered sugar 1 cup (100 g) at a time until creamy. Spread the frosting evenly over the top of your jelly layer.

Garnish the cake with chopped peanuts, if desired.

OATMEAL CREAM PIE COOKIE CAKE

If you're like me, then you've never had an oatmeal cream pie too far from reach. How about mega-sizing that treat and turning it into this giant Oatmeal Cream Pie Cookie Cake? A spiced oatmeal cookie cake is filled with a creamy and tasty marshmallow frosting, really encompassing the flavor of the classic snack.

SERVES 8 TO 10

1 cup (240 g) unsalted butter, softened

¾ cup (135 g) brown sugar

½ cup (100 g) granulated sugar

1 tbsp (15 ml) molasses

1½ tsp (8 ml) vanilla extract

2 eggs

1½ cups (180 g) all-purpose flour

½ tsp salt

1 tsp baking soda

½ tsp cinnamon

1½ cups (135 g) quick-cooking oats

FROSTING

1 cup (240 g) unsalted butter, softened

1 (7-oz [198-g]) jar marshmallow cream

2 cups (200 g) powdered sugar

1 tsp vanilla extract

Preheat the oven to 350°F (177°C, or gas mark 4). Line two 8-inch (20-cm) round baking pans with parchment paper, and spray with nonstick cooking spray. Set aside.

In a stand mixer, beat together your butter and both sugars until light and fluffy. Add in your molasses and vanilla, and mix until combined. Add in your eggs one at a time, mixing well after each addition.

In another bowl, whisk together your flour, salt, baking soda and cinnamon. Slowly add the dry mixture into your butter mixture, then mix in the oats. Spread the batter evenly into the prepared pans, and bake for 18 to 20 minutes. Remove the cakes from the oven and let them cool in the pans for 5 minutes before removing to wire racks to cool completely.

To make the frosting, in a stand mixer, beat together your butter and marshmallow cream until smooth. Add in your powdered sugar 1 cup (100 g) at a time until blended, then mix in the vanilla until incorporated.

To assemble the cake, place one layer onto a turntable or cake round. Spread your frosting over the top, then top with the remaining cake layer.

LEMON ZINGER CAKE

I have always been one to buy boxes upon boxes of zingers when I just so happen to go down the aisle at the grocery store. The vanilla zingers have been one of my favorite late night treats. How about adding a little lemon to the mix? A vanilla cake is filled with a fluffy marshmallow cream filling and frosted with a light lemon buttercream.

SERVES 12 TO 16

¾ cup (180 g) unsalted butter, softened

1½ cups (250 g) granulated sugar

3 eggs

2 tsp (10 ml) vanilla extract

2¼ cups (280 g) all-purpose flour

2 tsp (10 g) baking powder

½ tsp baking soda

1 tsp salt

1 cup (240 ml) milk

FILLING

½ cup (120 g) unsalted butter, softened

1 (7-oz [198-g]) container marshmallow cream

1 tsp vanilla extract

3 cups (300 g) powdered sugar

FROSTING

1½ cups (360 g) unsalted butter, softened

7 cups (700 g) powdered sugar

¼ cup (60 ml) lemon juice

Yellow food coloring

Preheat the oven to 350°F (177°C, or gas mark 4). Line two 9-inch (23-cm) cake pans with parchment paper and spray with nonstick cooking spray. Set aside.

In a stand mixer, beat together your butter and sugar until light and fluffy. Add in your eggs one at a time, mixing well after each addition, then mix in your vanilla until incorporated.

In another bowl, whisk together your flour, baking powder, baking soda and salt. Alternate adding the dry ingredients and milk into your butter mixture. Divide the batter evenly into the prepared pans, and bake for 25 to 30 minutes until golden and the cakes spring back when touched. Remove the cakes from the oven, and cool in the pans for 5 minutes before transferring to a wire rack to cool completely.

To make the filling, in a stand mixer, beat together your butter and marshmallow cream until combined. Add in your vanilla. Add in your powdered sugar 1 cup (100 g) at a time until combined.

To make the frosting, in a stand mixer, add your butter and beat until smooth. Add in the powdered sugar 1 cup (100 g) at a time until combined. Add in the lemon juice until blended. If the mixture is too wet, add more powdered sugar. Lastly, add in some drops of food coloring until the desired color is reached.

To assemble the cake, place one layer of the cake on a cake stand or turntable. Top with the filling and spread it out to the sides of the cake. Top with the remaining cake layer. Remove 1 cup (184 g) of the lemon frosting and set it aside, then frost the sides and top of cake.

Using an offset spatula, gently push into the frosting on sides and spin the cake around to create indents around the cake, moving up to the top of the cake. Place the reserved frosting in a piping bag fitted with an open star tip, and pipe swirls on top of the cake.

ROOT BEER FLOAT CAKE

Once that summer heat hits, root beer floats are in full swing in my house. With this Root Beer Float Cake, you can have that favorite summer drink all year round. A root beer–flavored cake is poked and poured with sweetened condensed milk and topped with whipped topping. This is an easy cake that will make the whole family happy.

SERVES 12 TO 15

1 (15.25-oz [432-g]) white cake mix

1 cup (240 ml) root beer

½ cup (120 ml) vegetable oil

3 eggs

1 tsp root beer extract

1 (14-oz [397-g]) can sweetened condensed milk

1 (8-oz [226-g]) container whipped topping

Preheat the oven to 350°F (177°C, or gas mark 4). Spray a 9 x 13–inch (23 x 33–cm) cake pan with nonstick cooking spray. Set aside.

In a large bowl, add your cake mix, root beer, vegetable oil, eggs and extract. Beat with a hand mixer for 2 minutes. Pour the batter into the prepared pan, and bake for 30 minutes until the center is set.

Remove the cake from the oven, and immediately poke holes in the top of the cake with the end of a wooden spoon. Pour your sweetened condensed milk over the top of the cake. Cover and refrigerate for 1 to 2 hours.

Spread the top with whipped topping.

BROWNIE COOKIE DOUGH CAKE

When I was growing up, my mom would get so mad at my dad and me because we stole all the cookie dough before she could actually make the cookies. With this Brownie Cookie Dough Cake, you get two giant brownies filled with cookie dough!

—————————————— SERVES 12 TO 16 ——————————————

1 cup (240 g) unsalted butter, softened

⅔ cup (85 g) unsweetened cocoa powder

2 cups (400 g) granulated sugar

4 eggs

1½ tsp (8 ml) vanilla extract

1 cup (120 g) all-purpose flour

½ tsp baking powder

½ tsp salt

FILLING

¾ cup (180 g) unsalted butter, softened

¾ cup (135 g) brown sugar

¾ cup (150 g) granulated sugar

3 tbsp (45 ml) milk

1½ tsp (8 ml) vanilla extract

1½ cups (180 g) all-purpose flour

1 cup (175 g) mini chocolate chips

GANACHE

1 (12-oz [340-g]) package semi-sweet chocolate chips

1 cup (240 ml) heavy cream

Mini chocolate chip cookies, for garnish

Image on page 12.

Preheat the oven to 350°F (177°C, or gas mark 4). Line two 8-inch (20-cm) round cake pans with parchment paper, and spray with nonstick cooking spray. Set aside.

Melt your butter in the microwave. Stir in your cocoa powder, then whisk in your sugar until blended. Whisk in your eggs one at a time, making sure to fully incorporate after each addition. Add in your vanilla.

In a small bowl, mix together your flour, baking powder and salt. Fold it into your chocolate mixture. Spread the batter into the prepared pans, and bake for 30 to 35 minutes or until the center is set. Remove the cakes from the oven, and let them cool slightly before turning them out onto a wire rack to cool completely.

To make the filling, in a stand mixer, beat together your butter and sugars until fluffy. Add in your milk and vanilla, and beat until smooth. Mix in the flour until combined, then fold in your chocolate chips.

To assemble the cake, place one layer of your brownie on a turntable or cake round. Press your filling mixture on top, and spread it out to fit the size of the brownie layer. Top with the second brownie layer, then place it in the refrigerator to chill.

To make the ganache, add your chocolate chips to a heat-safe bowl. Set aside. Add your heavy cream to a microwave-safe bowl, and heat it in the microwave for 1 to 2 minutes until bubbling. Remove from the microwave and pour over your chocolate chips. Let sit 5 to 7 minutes. After you let it sit, whisk the mixture together until smooth and let sit another 5 minutes to thicken slightly. Pour half of your ganache over the top of your cake, spread to the sides to drip down, and let set.

Place the remaining ganache in the refrigerator, and let it chill for 30 minutes. Once chilled, beat with a hand mixer for 3 to 5 minutes until light and fluffy. It will turn a light brown in color. Add your whipped ganache to a large piping bag fitted with an open star tip, and pipe swirls around the top of your cake. Top your swirls with mini chocolate chip cookies.

SNICKERDOODLE SHEET CAKE

Where are my cookie lovers at? Snickerdoodles are a family favorite. I grew up with my mom always making these iconic cookies. Soft and moist, they were always a go-to classic. This sheet cake has all the cinnamon and cream cheese flavors that you love in each and every fluffy bite.

SERVES 20 TO 24

1 cup (240 g) unsalted butter, softened

1 cup (240 ml) water

2 cups (240 g) all-purpose flour

2 cups (400 g) granulated sugar

2 eggs

½ cup (60 g) sour cream

2 tsp (10 ml) vanilla extract

1 tsp baking soda

1 tsp salt

1 tbsp (7 g) cinnamon

FROSTING

1 (8-oz [230-g]) package cream cheese, softened

½ cup (120 g) unsalted butter, softened

1 tsp vanilla extract

4 cups (400 g) powdered sugar

1 tsp cinnamon

TOPPING

2 tbsp (15 g) granulated sugar

½ tsp cinnamon

Preheat the oven to 375°F (190°C, or gas mark 5). Line a 12 x 17–inch (30 x 43–cm) or 15 x 10–inch (38 x 25–cm) baking sheet with parchment paper. Spray with nonstick cooking spray and set aside.

On the stove, melt together your butter and water. Set aside. In a stand mixer, mix together your flour and sugar until combined. Add in your eggs, sour cream, vanilla, baking soda and salt. Mix until smooth. Slowly pour in your melted butter and water mixture until combined, and beat until smooth. Lastly, add in your cinnamon and mix until incorporated.

Pour the batter into the prepared pan, and bake for 20 to 23 minutes until golden and the center is set, then remove the cake from the oven to cool completely.

To make the frosting, in a stand mixer, add your cream cheese, butter and vanilla, and beat until smooth. Add in your powdered sugar 1 cup (100 g) at a time until the desired consistency is reached. Add in your cinnamon and mix until incorporated. Spread evenly over the cooled cake.

To make the topping, mix together your sugar and cinnamon, and sprinkle over the top of the frosted cake.

CINNAMON ROLL SNACK CAKE

I love waking up in the mornings to a warm and gooey cinnamon roll. But I also love going to sleep with a delicious slice of cake. This Cinnamon Roll Snack Cake is swirled with the classic cinnamon roll filling, and baked up warm and tender. It's glazed with a traditional powdered sugar glaze, taking your normal morning routine into a favorite after-dinner snack.

—————————— SERVES 8 TO 10 ——————————

1 cup (200 g) granulated sugar

¼ cup (60 g) unsalted butter, softened

½ tsp salt

1 egg

1½ tsp (8 ml) vanilla extract

1½ cups (180 g) all-purpose flour

1½ tsp (6 g) baking powder

¾ cup (180 ml) milk

SWIRL

¼ cup (60 g) unsalted butter, melted

¼ cup (45 g) brown sugar

2 tsp (10 g) all-purpose flour

1½ tsp (6 g) cinnamon

1 tsp vanilla extract

GLAZE

1 cup (100 g) powdered sugar

2 tbsp (30 ml) milk

Preheat the oven to 350°F (177°C, or gas mark 4). Layer a 9-inch (23-cm) springform pan with parchment paper and spray with nonstick cooking spray. Set aside.

In a large bowl, beat together the sugar, butter and salt with a hand mixer until light and fluffy. Add in your egg and vanilla, and mix until blended.

In another bowl, whisk together your flour and baking powder. Add this to your wet ingredients and blend until just incorporated. Slowly add in your milk and continue beating until combined. Spread the batter into the prepared pan. Set aside.

To make the swirl, in a bowl, mix together your butter, brown sugar, flour, cinnamon and vanilla until smooth. Drizzle the mixture over your cake batter and, using a knife, swirl it into the batter until combined. Bake in the oven for 30 to 35 minutes until golden and a toothpick inserted in the center of the cake comes out clean. Let it cool for about 10 minutes before removing it from the pan.

To make the glaze, in a bowl, whisk together the powdered sugar and milk until combined and smooth. Pour it over the slightly cooled cake.

EXTRAORDINARY
CHEESECAKES AND PIES

In this chapter you'll find a variety of no-bake and baked treats that are as fun to make as they are to eat. Pies and cheesecakes are well known, and these recipes give them exciting new twists—from an Apple Crisp Cheesecake (page 55) to a Strawberry Daiquiri Pie (page 43). You'll have fun whipping up these untraditional treats!

CHURRO CHEESECAKE

With hints of cinnamon and sugar, this Churro Cheesecake is a no-bake cheesecake with a snickerdoodle cookie crust. Creamy, with a little bit of spice, this cheesecake creates a flavor explosion that keeps you coming back for another bite.

SERVES 8 TO 10

CRUST

¼ cup (60 g) unsalted butter, softened

½ cup (100 g) plus 1 tbsp (13 g) granulated sugar, divided

1 egg yolk

½ tsp vanilla extract

¾ (90 g) cup all-purpose flour

¼ tsp baking soda

⅛ tsp cream of tartar

¼ tsp salt

½ tsp cinnamon, divided

CHEESECAKE LAYER

3 (8-oz [690-g]) packages cream cheese, softened

1¼ cups (125 g) powdered sugar, divided

1 tbsp (15 ml) vanilla extract

2 tsp (5 g) cinnamon, divided

1 cup (240 ml) heavy cream

2 tbsp (25 g) granulated sugar

Preheat the oven to 350°F (177°C, or gas mark 4). Spray a 9-inch (23-cm) springform pan with nonstick cooking spray. Set aside.

In a stand mixer, beat together your butter and ½ cup (100 g) of sugar until fluffy. Add in your egg yolk and vanilla, and mix until combined. Add in the flour, baking soda, cream of tartar, salt and ¼ teaspoon of cinnamon, and mix until the dough comes together.

Press your dough into the prepared pan. In a small bowl, mix together your remaining sugar and cinnamon. Sprinkle the cinnamon-sugar mixture over top of the prepared dough. Bake for 12 to 15 minutes until just set, leaving it a little underdone. Remove the crust from the oven, and let it cool completely.

To make the cheesecake layer, in a stand mixer on medium speed, beat your cream cheese until smooth. Add in 1 cup (100 g) of powdered sugar, vanilla and 1 teaspoon of cinnamon. Mix until blended and creamy.

In a medium bowl, beat together your heavy cream and ¼ cup (25 g) of powdered sugar with a hand mixer until stiff peaks form. Fold it into your cream cheese mixture, and spread the mixture over the cooled crust.

In a small bowl, mix together your granulated sugar and remaining cinnamon, and sprinkle over the top of the cheesecake. Cover and chill for 3 to 4 hours or until set.

STRAWBERRY DAIQUIRI PIE

Love the drink of the same name? This pie is filled with a tart and sweet strawberry flavor that is set off by hints of lime, making this no-bake pie a refreshing treat.

SERVES 8 TO 10

1 (8-oz [230-g]) package cream cheese, softened

1 (14-oz [396-g]) can sweetened condensed milk

6 oz (180 ml) strawberry daiquiri concentrate, thawed

3 cups (225 g) whipped topping, divided

1 (9-inch [23-cm]) premade graham cracker crust

Lime zest, for garnish

Strawberries, for garnish

In a stand mixer, beat your cream cheese until smooth. Mix in your sweetened condensed milk and strawberry daiquiri concentrate until combined. Fold in 2 cups (246 g) of your whipped topping, then spread the mixture into the crust.

Cover and freeze for 6 to 8 hours. Top with the remaining whipped topping, creating swirls. Add lime zest and strawberries, if desired.

CINNAMON CRUNCH CEREAL PIE

A simple pie with so much flavor. This pie is a no-bake hit around our house. Take the subtle flavors of our favorite cereal soaked in milk, add a little pudding and whipped topping and spread it into a graham cracker crust, and you have a pie that will bring out the kid in you.

SERVES 8 TO 10

4 cups (340 g) cinnamon cereal such as Cinnamon Toast Crunch, divided

2 cups (475 ml) milk

1 (3.4-oz [96-g]) package vanilla pudding

1 (8-oz [230-g]) container whipped topping, plus extra for topping (optional)

1 (9-inch [23-cm]) premade graham cracker crust

Add 3 cups (255 g) of the cereal to a large bowl, pour your milk over the top and stir around to cover. Let sit for about 20 minutes, then strain your cereal milk mixture into another bowl. Press the cereal with a spatula to get out any excess milk, then discard the cereal.

Whisk the pudding into the milk until thickened, then fold in your whipped topping.

Spread the mixture into the graham cracker crust. Cover and refrigerate for 3 to 4 hours until set.

Once set, crush the remaining cup (85 g) of cereal and sprinkle it over the top of the pie. Garnish with extra whipped topping, if desired.

CRÈME BRÛLÉE CHEESECAKE

Crème brûlée makes me feel fancy, but this cheesecake takes little effort—and makes people feel like you spent hours creating a masterpiece. A creamy cheesecake is baked up and refrigerated, then topped with sugar and torched until it becomes golden and hard.

SERVES 8 TO 10

CRUST

2 cups (180 g) graham cracker crumbs

¼ cup (50 g) granulated sugar

7 tbsp (105 g) butter, melted

CHEESECAKE

3 (8-oz [230-g]) packages cream cheese, softened

1 cup (200 g) granulated sugar

1 cup (120 g) sour cream

3 eggs

2 tsp (10 ml) vanilla extract

TOPPING

2 tbsp (25 g) granulated sugar

Preheat the oven to 350°F (177°C, or gas mark 4). Spray a 9-inch (23-cm) springform pan with nonstick cooking spray. Wrap the bottom and sides of the pan with heavy-duty tin foil. Set aside.

To make the crust, in a bowl, mix together the graham cracker crumbs, sugar and butter until combined. Pour the mixture into the prepared pan, and press onto the bottom and up the sides. Set aside.

In a stand mixer, beat your cream cheese until smooth. Add in your sugar, and beat until blended. Add in your sour cream, and mix until incorporated. Add in the eggs one at a time, mixing well after each addition. Lastly, add in your vanilla until incorporated. Pour the cheesecake into the prepared crust.

Place your springform pan in a large roasting pan and fill with hot water until it's halfway up the sides. Place the pan in the oven and bake the cheesecake for 1 hour and 10 minutes, until the center is just set. Turn off the heat and crack the oven door. Let the cheesecake cool like this for 1 hour, then remove the cheesecake from the oven and let it cool to room temperature. Cover and refrigerate for 8 hours.

When ready to serve, sprinkle the sugar over the top of the cheesecake. Using a kitchen torch, heat the sugar until golden and glass-like.

CHOCOLATE NOUGAT CANDY BAR PIE

The traditional potluck favorite has gotten a makeover! This candy bar pie, full of diced apples and Snickers all in a creamy filling, is a fun no-bake spin on a classic salad, thrown into a pie crust and served in slices. Whip out your forks, people, because this stuff is good!

SERVES 8 TO 10

CRUST

2 cups (180 g) graham cracker crumbs

¼ cup (50 g) granulated sugar

8 tbsp (120 g) unsalted butter, melted

FILLING

8 oz (225 g) cream cheese, softened

1 (3.4-oz [96-g]) box vanilla pudding

1 cup (240 ml) milk

2 (8-oz [226-g]) containers whipped topping, divided

1 large Granny Smith apple, cored and chopped

2 king-size Snickers bars, chopped and divided

Caramel sauce, for garnish (optional)

To make the crust, add your graham cracker crumbs, sugar and melted butter in a medium bowl. Stir together until combined and all of the crumbs are moist. Add the crumbs into a 9-inch (23-cm) pie pan, and press firmly against the bottom and sides of pan to form a crust. Refrigerate the crust.

To make the filling, beat your cream cheese in a large bowl with an electric mixer until smooth. Add in your vanilla pudding and milk, and continue to beat until blended and slightly thickened. Fold in one 8-ounce (226-g) container of whipped topping until combined. Mix in the apple and all but a ½ cup (85 g) of chopped Snickers bars and stir until just incorporated. Spoon the filling into your prepared crust. Cover and refrigerate for 3 hours or until thickened.

Remove the pie from the refrigerator and top with the remaining 8 ounces (226 g) of whipped topping. Sprinkle the pie with the remaining Snickers bars and drizzle with caramel sauce, if desired.

COCONUT MACAROON PIE

Growing up, we always had coconut macaroons around my house. The flavor of the delicious coconut and chocolate is almost irresistible. This pie is pretty much one giant cookie. A flavorful, sweet, coconut filling drizzled with a light and crunchy chocolate topping make this pie a large-and-in-charge version of the classic handheld treat.

SERVES 8 TO 10

1 (9-inch [23-cm]) refrigerated pie crust

½ cup (120 g) unsalted butter, melted

2 eggs

1½ cups (300 g) granulated sugar

½ cup (30 g) all-purpose flour

¼ cup (60 ml) water

1 tbsp (15 ml) white vinegar

½ tsp coconut extract

1 tsp vanilla extract

1½ cups (110 g) shredded coconut

TOPPING

¼ cup (45 g) semi-sweet chocolate chips

¼ tsp vegetable oil

Preheat the oven to 350°F (177°C, or gas mark 4). On a lightly-floured surface, lightly roll out the pie crust. Place it in a 9-inch (23-cm) pie plate. Set aside.

In a large bowl, whisk together your butter, eggs, sugar, flour, water, vinegar and extracts until smooth. Fold in your coconut. Pour the mixture into the prepared pie crust, and bake in the oven for 40 to 45 minutes until golden. Remove the pie from the oven, and let it cool completely on the counter. Refrigerate for 1 to 2 hours until set.

To make the topping, add your chocolate chips and vegetable oil to a microwave-safe bowl. Heat in the microwave for 1 minute, stirring after 30 seconds. Drizzle over the cooled pie.

OATMEAL CREAM PIE CHEESECAKE

One of my favorite after-school snacks growing up was the iconic oatmeal cream pie: the soft sandwich cookies encasing that creamy irresistible filling. Now take that times 10 for this no-bake cheesecake. Oatmeal cream pies create the crust of this marshmallow-spiked cheesecake making it the cheesecake of every kid's dreams.

— SERVES 8 TO 10 —

FILLING

1 (10-oz [283-g]) bag mini marshmallows

¾ cup (180 ml) milk

3 (8-oz [230-g]) packages cream cheese, softened

1 (8-oz [226-g]) container whipped topping, plus extra for garnish

1 (12-count) box oatmeal cream pies, reserve some for garnish

In a large saucepan, melt together your mini marshmallows and milk until smooth. Pour it into a bowl, and set aside to cool.

While the marshmallow cools, spray the bottom and sides of a 9-inch (23-cm) springform pan with nonstick cooking spray. Unwrap your oatmeal cream pies and press them onto the bottom and up the sides of the pan about 1 inch (2.5 cm). Set aside.

In a stand mixer, beat your cream cheese until smooth. Add in your cooled marshmallow mixture, and beat until incorporated. Fold in your whipped topping until incorporated. Spread the mixture into the prepared crust, and refrigerate 6 to 8 hours until set. Top with whipped topping and quartered oatmeal cream pies, if desired.

APPLE CRISP CHEESECAKE

I grew up eating apple crisp because we had apples to spare almost every single year. Cheesecake is one of my favorite desserts as well, and combining the two classics together was a no-brainer. Diced fresh apples line the bottom of this creamy cheesecake. Topped with a crunchy oat topping, this cheesecake has all your favorite flavors in one dessert.

SERVES 8 TO 10

CRUST

2 cups (180 g) graham cracker crumbs

¼ cup (50 g) granulated sugar

7 tbsp (105 g) unsalted butter, melted

CHEESECAKE

3 (8-oz [230-g]) packages cream cheese, softened

1 cup (120 g) sour cream

2½ tsp (12 ml) vanilla extract

3 eggs

3 cups (450 g) apple, peeled, cored and sliced ¼ inch (6 mm) thin

1 tsp cinnamon

1 tsp salt

2 tbsp (25 g) granulated sugar

TOPPING

¼ cup (30 g) all-purpose flour

¼ cup (22 g) old-fashioned oats

¼ cup (45 g) brown sugar

1 tsp cinnamon

2 tbsp (30 g) butter, softened

Preheat the oven to 350°F (177°C, or gas mark 4). Line a 9-inch (23-cm) springform pan with parchment paper and wrap the bottom and sides of the pan with heavy-duty tin foil. Set aside.

To make the crust, in a large bowl, mix together your graham cracker crumbs, sugar and melted butter until combined. Press the crust into the bottom and up the sides of the prepared pan and set aside.

In a stand mixer, add your cream cheese and on medium speed, mix until smooth. Add in your sour cream and vanilla until combined. Add in your eggs one at a time, making sure the eggs are incorporated after each addition.

In a large bowl, add your apples, cinnamon, salt and sugar. Toss to coat. Layer the apples on top of the crust, covering it evenly. Pour your cheesecake filling over the top of apples. Set aside.

To make the topping, in a medium bowl, mix together your flour, oats, brown sugar, cinnamon and butter until pea-sized crumbs form. Sprinkle over the cheesecake.

Place your springform pan in a large roasting pan, and fill halfway up the sides with hot water. Place in the oven and bake for 1 hour and 10 minutes, until the center is just set.

Turn off the heat and crack the oven door open. Let it cool this way for 1 hour. Remove the cheesecake from the oven, and let it cool completely. Cover and refrigerate for 8 hours.

BOSTON CREAM PIE CHEESECAKE

As one of my favorite cakes, Boston cream pie has long been a flavor that I enjoy in any way, shape or form. This cheesecake is three layers of deliciousness: a moist cake bottom, a cheesecake center and a chocolate ganache topping. There is no resisting these three different textures that you get in each and every bite.

SERVES 8 TO 10

CAKE LAYER

¼ cup (120 g) unsalted butter, softened

½ cup (100 g) granulated sugar

¼ cup (30 g) sour cream

1 tsp vanilla extract

1 egg

¾ cup (90 g) all-purpose flour

½ tsp salt

1 tsp baking powder

¼ cup (60 ml) milk

CHEESECAKE LAYER

2 (8-oz [230-g]) packages cream cheese, softened

2 (3.4-oz [96-g]) packages vanilla pudding

1 cup (240 ml) milk

1 tsp vanilla extract

1 cup (100 g) powdered sugar

2 cups (150 g) whipped topping

GANACHE

½ cup (75 g) semi-sweet chocolate chips

¼ cup (60 ml) heavy cream

Preheat the oven to 350°F (177°C, or gas mark 4). Line a 9-inch (23-cm) springform pan with parchment paper. Set aside.

In a large bowl, beat together your butter and sugar with a hand mixer until light and fluffy. Add in your sour cream, vanilla and egg, and beat until combined.

In a small bowl, whisk together your flour, salt and baking powder. Slowly mix it into your butter mixture until just incorporated, then slowly beat in your milk. Spread the batter into the prepared pan, and bake for 15 to 20 minutes until set. Remove the cake from the oven, and let it cool completely.

To make the cheesecake filling, in a stand mixer, beat your cream cheese until smooth. Add in your pudding mixture and milk, and continue to beat until blended. Add in the vanilla and powdered sugar until just combined, then fold in your whipped topping. Spread it into the cooled crust. Cover and refrigerate for 3 to 4 hours.

To make the ganache topping, add your chocolate chips to a heat-safe bowl. In a microwave-safe bowl, add your cream and heat it in the microwave until bubbling, about 1 minute. Pour the cream over the chocolate chips, and let sit for 5 minutes. Whisk the mixture until smooth, then pour it over the chilled cheesecake. Let the topping set for 10 minutes.

PEANUT BUTTER AND JELLY PIE

I was a kid who grew up eating all the peanut butter and jelly sandwiches I could handle. It's become a favorite memory of my youth, so why not kick it up a notch and create a fun flavorful pie with the same delicious flavors? A flaky pie crust is filled with a creamy peanut butter filling, topped with a layer of jelly, and finished off with a light whipped cream topping and chopped peanuts. This is the adult version of your favorite sandwich.

SERVES 8 TO 10

1 (9-inch [23-cm]) refrigerated pie crust

1 (8-oz [230-g]) package cream cheese

⅔ cup (120 g) peanut butter

½ cup (50 g) powdered sugar

2 tbsp (30 ml) milk

¾ cup (245 g) grape jelly

1 (8-oz [230-g]) container whipped topping

Preheat the oven to 450°F (232°C). Place your pie crust on a lightly-floured cutting board and gently roll it out slightly. Press the crust into the bottom and up the sides of a 9-inch (23-cm) deep-dish pie plate. Poke holes in the bottom and sides, and bake in the oven for 11 to 13 minutes until golden, then remove. Set aside to cool.

To make the peanut butter layer, in a stand mixer, beat your cream cheese until smooth. Add in your peanut butter, powdered sugar and milk, and beat until creamy. Spread into the cooled crust.

Add your grape jelly to a bowl, and whisk to break up the lumps. Spread the jelly on top of your peanut butter layer. Then spread your whipped topping over the jelly layer. Refrigerate for at least 1 hour before serving.

BLUEBERRY MUFFIN CHEESECAKE

Breakfast for dessert? Who can resist? Growing up, blueberry muffins were my favorite breakfast of choice. This creamy cheesecake is full of fresh blueberries, topped with a crunchy streusel topping and finished off with a delicious powdered sugar glaze. This cheesecake will be hard to save for just dessert.

SERVES 8 TO 10

CRUST

2 cups (180 g) graham cracker crumbs

¼ cup (50 g) granulated sugar

7 tbsp (105 g) butter, melted

CHEESECAKE

3 (8-oz [230-g]) packages cream cheese, softened

1 cup (120 g) sour cream

2½ tsp (13 ml) vanilla extract

3 eggs

1½ cups (340 g) blueberries

1 tbsp (8 g) all-purpose flour

TOPPING

¾ cup (150 g) granulated sugar

½ cup (60 g) flour

1 tsp cinnamon

6 tbsp (85 g) unsalted butter, softened

GLAZE

1 tbsp (15 g) unsalted butter, melted

½ cup (50 g) powdered sugar

3–4 tsp (15–20 ml) milk

Preheat the oven to 350°F (177°C, or gas mark 4). Line a 9-inch (23-cm) springform pan with parchment paper and wrap the bottom and sides with heavy-duty tin foil. Set aside.

In a medium bowl, mix together your graham cracker crumbs, sugar and butter until combined. Press the mixture into the bottom and up the sides of the prepared pan. Set aside.

In a stand mixer, add your cream cheese and beat on medium speed until smooth. Add in your sour cream and vanilla until blended. Add in your eggs one at a time, making sure they are incorporated after each addition.

In a medium bowl, toss together your blueberries and flour until coated. Fold the berries into the cheesecake batter, then pour the batter into the prepared crust.

In another medium bowl, add all of your topping ingredients. Blend together with a pastry blender until pea-sized crumbs form. Sprinkle on top of your cheesecake mixture.

Place your springform pan in a large roasting pan, and fill with water halfway up the sides. Place the pan in the oven and bake for 1 hour and 10 minutes, until the center is just set.

Turn off the heat and crack the oven door open. Let cool for 1 hour. Remove the cheesecake from the oven, and let it cool completely. Cover and refrigerate for 8 hours.

To make the glaze, mix together your butter, powdered sugar and milk. Drizzle it over the top of the cooled cheesecake before serving.

MARSHMALLOW PEANUT BUTTER COOKIE PIE

Is it a cookie or a pie? How about a little bit of both? A peanut butter cookie dough is folded with marshmallows, spread into a flaky pie crust and baked until gooey and delicious. With bits of marshmallow in each and every bite, this pie combines two delicious flavors into one tasty dessert.

SERVES 8 TO 10

1 (9-inch [23-cm]) refrigerated pie crust

½ cup (120 g) unsalted butter, softened

¾ cup (135 g) creamy peanut butter

½ cup (90 g) brown sugar

½ cup (100 g) granulated sugar

1 egg

1½ tsp (8 ml) vanilla extract

1 tbsp (15 ml) milk

½ tsp salt

1½ cups (180 g) flour

1½ cups (75 g) mini marshmallows

Preheat the oven to 350°F (177°F, or gas mark 4). On a lightly-floured surface, gently roll out the pie crust slightly. Press it into a 9-inch (23-cm) deep-dish pie plate. Set aside.

In a stand mixer, beat together your butter, peanut butter and both sugars until combined. Add in your egg, vanilla, milk and salt, and mix until incorporated. Slowly add in the flour until the mixture comes together, then fold in the mini marshmallows. Press into the pie crust and bake for 35 minutes until the center is just set.

Remove the cookie pie from the oven, and cool completely before serving.

SNICKERS SLAB PIE

Candy bar fan? I know I am! This pie literally is all that and a bag of chips. A flaky pie crust is layered with caramel, nougat and chocolate just like the classic candy bar. Better yet, this pie can be eaten in handheld form.

SERVES 12 TO 15

CRUST

1 (9-inch [23-cm]) refrigerated pie crust

NOUGAT LAYER

1¼ cups (250 g) granulated sugar

½ cup (120 ml) evaporated milk

⅓ cup (80 g) unsalted butter

¼ cup (45 g) creamy peanut butter

1 (7-oz [198-g]) container marshmallow fluff

CARAMEL LAYER

1 (11-oz [311-g]) bag caramels or caramel bits

2 tbsp (30 ml) sweetened condensed milk

CANDY BAR LAYER

1¼ cups (220 g) semi-sweet chocolate chips

¼ cup (45 g) creamy peanut butter

Preheat the oven to 450°F (232°C, or gas mark 8). On a lightly-floured surface, gently roll your pie crust into a large 10 x 14–inch (25 x 35–cm) rectangle. Press it into the bottom and up the sides of a 9 x 13 x 1–inch (23 x 33 x 3–cm) bar pan. Prick holes in the bottom of the pie crust. Bake in the oven for 11 to 13 minutes or until golden. Remove and set aside to cool.

To make the nougat layer, in a saucepan, mix together your sugar, evaporated milk and butter. Bring it to a boil and let the mixture boil for 5 minutes without stirring. Remove from the heat, and stir in your peanut butter and marshmallow fluff until blended and creamy. Spread the mixture into the pie crust, and place it in the refrigerator to set.

To make the caramel layer, in a microwave-safe bowl, add together your caramels and sweetened condensed milk. Heat in the microwave for 2 minutes, stirring every 30 seconds until melted. Remove your pie crust from the refrigerator. Pour the caramel over the nougat layer, then return it to the refrigerator.

Lastly, to make the candy bar layer, in a microwave-safe bowl, add your chocolate chips and peanut butter. Heat in the microwave for 1 to 2 minutes, stirring every 30 seconds until melted. Spread over the caramel layer and place back in refrigerator to set, around 30 minutes.

BANANA CREAM PIE CHEESECAKE

If I could eat a banana-flavored dessert every day of my life, I would. Banana cream pie has always been one of my absolute favorite pies, so why not make it into a cheesecake? Bananas and vanilla wafers are layered with a creamy, banana-flavored cheesecake filling, making each and every bite more flavorful than the one before.

–––––––––––––– SERVES 8 TO 10 ––––––––––––––

CRUST

2 cups (180 g) graham cracker crumbs

¼ cup (50 g) granulated sugar

7 tbsp (105 g) unsalted butter, melted

FILLING

2 (8-oz [230-g]) packages cream cheese, softened

1 (3.4-oz [96-g]) package banana pudding

½ cup (50 g) powdered sugar

½ cup (120 ml) milk

1 (8-oz [226-g]) container whipped topping

2 large bananas, sliced, plus more for garnish

1–2 cups (160–320 g) vanilla wafers

Whipped topping, for garnish

To make the crust, mix together your graham cracker crumbs, sugar and butter. Press it into the bottom and up the sides of a 9-inch (23-cm) springform pan. Set aside.

In a stand mixer, beat your cream cheese until smooth. Add in your pudding and beat until combined. Mix in the powdered sugar, milk and whipped topping until light and fluffy. Spread half of your filling mixture into the prepared crust. Top with vanilla wafers and sliced bananas followed by the remaining filling mixture. Refrigerate for 4 to 6 hours until set. Top with whipped topping and sliced bananas, if desired.

CHOCOLATE CHIP COOKIE PIE

I love cookies and I love pie, so why not mash the two together and create a warm, gooey cookie pie? This Chocolate Chip Cookie Pie is literally an amped-up version of your favorite cookie but eaten with a fork. Bigger portions in every single bite.

———————————————— SERVES 8 TO 10 ————————————————

2 eggs

½ cup (60 g) all-purpose flour

¾ cup (135 g) brown sugar

⅓ cup (65 g) granulated sugar

¾ cup (180 g) unsalted butter, softened

½ tsp salt

1 tsp vanilla extract

1½ cups (265 g) semi-sweet chocolate chips

1 (9-inch [23-cm]) frozen deep-dish pie crust, thawed

Preheat the oven to 325°F (163°C, or gas mark 3).

In a stand mixer, beat your eggs until foamy and pale yellow. Add in your flour, brown sugar and granulated sugar, and mix until combined. Add in your butter, salt and vanilla. Beat until incorporated, then fold in your chocolate chips.

Spoon the filling into the prepared pie crust. Bake in the oven for 60 minutes until a toothpick inserted in the center comes out clean. If the edges are browning too quickly, cover with tinfoil or pie crust shields.

TASTY TAKE-ALONG

BARS, BROWNIES AND BLONDIES

You can't go wrong with handheld treats. Bars, brownies and blondies are an essential part of baking. They are the perfect dish to bring along to picnics, potlucks or family get-togethers. In this chapter, you'll find everything from Muddy Buddy Brownies (page 86) to Banana Split Blondies (page 89). Fun, flavorful, take-along treats for everyone!

MINT CHOCOLATE CRISPY TREATS

Rice Krispies Treats have always been a staple treat in almost every kid's house. This Thin Mint version takes one of your favorite Girl Scout cookies and gives this classic treat a really flavorful twist.

———————————— MAKES 12 ————————————

½ cup (120 g) unsalted butter

1 (10.5-oz [298-g]) bag mini marshmallows

½ tsp mint extract

Green food coloring

6 cups (150 g) rice cereal, such as Rice Krispies

GANACHE

1¾ cups (305 g) semi-sweet chocolate chips

½ cup (120 ml) heavy cream

Spray a 9 x 13–inch (23 x 33–cm) pan with nonstick cooking spray. Set aside.

Melt the butter in a large saucepan, about 1 to 2 minutes. Add in your marshmallows and melt, stirring frequently. Once melted, remove from the heat, and stir in your extract and food coloring.

Add your rice cereal to a large bowl, and fold in your marshmallow mixture. Stir to combine, then press into the prepared pan.

To make the ganache, add your chocolate chips to a heat-safe bowl. Set aside. Add your heavy cream to a microwave-safe bowl. Heat in the microwave until bubbling, about 1 minute. Pour over your chocolate chips, and let sit for 5 to 7 minutes. Whisk together your cream and chocolate until smooth, then pour and spread over your bars.

Refrigerate for 30 minutes until the topping is set.

CARROT CAKE BLONDIES

Carrot cake is a spring delight, but sometimes you want something just a little bit different. These blondies are full of all the cake flavors packed into a moist and delicious bar. Topped with a cream cheese frosting and sprinkled with chopped pecans, you will love these flavorful blondies.

───────── MAKES 12 TO 16 ─────────

1 cup (240 g) unsalted butter, melted

2 cups (360 g) brown sugar

3 tsp (15 ml) vanilla extract

2 eggs

2 cups (240 g) all-purpose flour

2 tsp (5 g) ground cinnamon

1 tsp ground ginger

1½ tsp (8 g) salt

2 cups (220 g) shredded carrots

1 cup (150 g) chopped pecans

FROSTING

½ cup (120 g) unsalted butter, softened

1 (8-oz [230-g]) package cream cheese, softened

2 tsp (10 ml) vanilla extract

4 cups (400 g) powdered sugar

½ cup (75 g) chopped pecans, for garnish

Preheat the oven to 350°F (177°C, or gas mark 4). Line a 9 x 13-inch (23 x 33-cm) baking dish with nonstick cooking spray. Set aside.

In a stand mixer, mix together your butter, brown sugar and vanilla until fluffy. Add in your eggs and mix well, then mix in your flour, cinnamon, ginger and salt. Lastly, add in your carrots and pecans until just combined. Spread it into the prepared pan and bake for 30 to 35 minutes until the center is just set. Remove the blondies from the oven, and let them cool.

To make the frosting, in a stand mixer, beat together your butter and cream cheese until smooth. Add in your vanilla until blended. Add your powder sugar 1 cup (100 g) at a time until the desired consistency is reached. Spread the frosting over the cooled bars, and sprinkle with chopped pecans.

COCONUT CREAM BLONDIES

If you're already a fan of blondies, then this coconut cream version will make you an even bigger one. With a chewy and delicious crust that is topped with a coconut cream cheese frosting, you can't go wrong with these unique and flavorful treats.

MAKES 12 TO 16

½ cup (120 g) unsalted butter

1½ cups (265 g) white chocolate chips

1¼ cups (150 g) all-purpose flour

¾ cup (150 g) granulated sugar

1 tsp vanilla extract

½ tsp salt

3 eggs

¾ cup (60 g) sweetened shredded coconut

FROSTING

1 (8-oz [230-g]) package cream cheese, softened

4 tbsp (60 g) unsalted butter, softened

¼ cup (60 ml) coconut milk

1 tsp vanilla extract

½ tsp coconut extract

3 cups (300 g) powdered sugar

½ cup (50 g) toasted coconut

Preheat the oven to 350°F (177°C, or gas mark 4). Spray a 9 x 13–inch (23 x 33–cm) baking dish with nonstick cooking spray. Set aside.

In a microwave-safe bowl, melt together your butter and white chocolate chips until smooth. Stir in your flour, sugar, vanilla, salt, eggs and coconut until combined. Pour the batter into the prepared pan, and bake for 30 minutes or until slightly golden. Set aside to cool completely.

To make the frosting, in a stand mixer, beat together the cream cheese and butter until smooth and combined. Add in your coconut milk, vanilla and coconut extract. Continue to mix until incorporated, then add in your powdered sugar 1 cup (100 g) at a time until you reach your desired consistency. Spread it over the cooled bars and top with toasted coconut.

CHOCOLATE SHEET CAKE BARS

If you're a fan of Texas sheet cake—which is a light and moist chocolate cake topped with a warm chocolate frosting—then you'll love these Chocolate Sheet Cake Bars. A dense and thick chocolate-flavored bar is topped with a poured chocolate frosting that makes these a double whammy when it comes to chocolate explosion.

MAKES 12

½ cup (120 g) unsalted butter, softened

½ cup (90 g) brown sugar

½ cup (100 g) granulated sugar

1 egg

1 tsp vanilla extract

1 tsp almond extract

¼ cup (30 g) sour cream

2 cups (240 g) all-purpose flour

½ cup (50 g) unsweetened cocoa powder

½ tsp baking powder

½ tsp baking soda

1 tsp salt

FROSTING

7 tbsp (105 g) unsalted butter

2 tbsp (15 g) unsweetened cocoa powder

3 tbsp (45 ml) milk

1 tsp vanilla extract

2 cups (200 g) powdered sugar

Preheat the oven to 350°F (177°C, or gas mark 4). Spray a 9 x 13–inch (23 x 33–cm) pan with nonstick cooking spray. Set aside.

In a large bowl, beat together your butter and both sugars with a hand mixer until fluffy. Add in your egg, extracts and sour cream, and mix until combined.

In a small bowl, sift together your flour, cocoa powder, baking powder, baking soda and salt until combined. Mix into your butter mixture, and beat with a hand mixer until blended. Press the mixture into the prepared pan, and bake for 20 to 25 minutes.

To make the frosting, in a saucepan on the stove, melt your butter over medium heat, about 1 to 2 minutes. Whisk in your cocoa powder, milk and vanilla until combined. Then remove from the heat, and whisk in your powdered sugar.

Once the bars are finished baking, immediately pour the frosting over the top of the bars. Cool for 30 minutes to let the frosting set up.

SUGAR COOKIE BROWNIES

Can't decide if you want cookies or brownies? Why not have both? These delicious fudge brownies are topped with sugar cookie pieces, giving you a gooey and crunchy texture with each and every bite.

―――――――――――――――― MAKES 12 TO 16 ――――――――――――――――

1 cup (240 g) unsalted butter

¾ cup (130 g) semi-sweet chocolate chips

1½ cups (300 g) granulated sugar

½ cup (90 g) brown sugar

4 eggs

2 tsp (10 ml) vanilla extract

¾ cup (95 g) cocoa powder

1 cup (120 g) all-purpose flour

1 tsp salt

¾ tsp baking powder

½ (16-oz [450-g]) sleeve of sugar cookie dough

Preheat the oven to 350°C (177°C, or gas mark 4). Line a 9 x 13–inch (23 x 33–cm) pan with parchment paper. Set aside.

In a medium microwave-safe bowl, add the butter and chocolate chips. Heat in the microwave for about 2 minutes, stirring every 30 seconds until combined. Whisk in the granulated and brown sugar until combined. Then whisk in your eggs one by one, mixing well after each addition. Add in your vanilla.

In a large bowl, add your cocoa powder, flour, salt and baking powder, and whisk together until combined. Slowly add in your wet ingredients to your dry ingredients, mixing until just blended, then pour the batter into the prepared pan.

Dollop your cookie dough over the top in about 1-tablespoon (15-g) measurements, then bake for 30 to 35 minutes. Remove the brownies from the oven, and cool them completely.

Image on page 70.

GLAZED OATMEAL RAISIN COOKIE BARS

Oatmeal Raisin Cookies are one of my absolute favorite cookies around, but we got bored with the normal cookie routine and decided that a bar of the same name would be better! Soft, moist and packed full of flavor, these are glazed and topped just like the classic version.

MAKES 12 TO 15
---

1 cup (240 g) unsalted butter, softened

¾ cup (135 g) brown sugar

¾ cup (150 g) granulated sugar

2 cups (180 g) old-fashioned oats

1½ cups (180 g) all-purpose flour

1 tsp baking powder

1 tsp salt

2 eggs

2 tsp (10 ml) vanilla extract

2 cups (300 g) raisins

GLAZE

2 cups (200 g) powdered sugar

2–3 tbsp (30–45 ml) heavy cream

Preheat the oven to 350°F (177°C, or gas mark 4). Line a 9 x 13-inch (23 x 33-cm) baking pan with parchment paper. Set aside.

In a stand mixer, cream together the butter and sugars until light and fluffy. Add in the oats, flour, baking powder and salt until combined. Then add in your eggs, vanilla and raisins, and mix until incorporated. Press the mixture into the prepared pan, and bake for 30 to 35 minutes until the center is set. Remove the bars from the oven to cool completely.

To make the glaze, whisk together the powdered sugar and cream until smooth, then pour it over the cooled bars.

STRAWBERRY SHORTCAKE BARS

If you love the traditional shortcakes, you'll fall in love with these Strawberry Shortcake Bars!
A shortbread crust is topped with a cream cheese frosting and covered in fresh strawberries.

—————————————————— MAKES 12 ——————————————————

CRUST

1 cup (240 g) unsalted butter, softened

½ cup (100 g) granulated sugar

2 cups (240 g) all-purpose flour

¼ tsp salt

TOPPING

1 (8-oz [230-g]) package cream cheese, softened

½ cup (50 g) powdered sugar

1 tsp vanilla extract

2 cups (150 g) whipped topping

1–1½ cups (200–300 g) diced strawberries

Preheat the oven to 350°F (177°C, or gas mark 4). Line a 9 x 9-inch (23 x 23-cm) pan with parchment paper. Set aside

In a food processor, add your butter, sugar, flour and salt. Process until crumbs form. Dump them out into the prepared pan and press down to form a crust. Bake for 25 minutes until the edges start to brown. Remove the bars from the oven, and let them cool completely.

With a hand mixer, beat your cream cheese and powdered sugar together until smooth. Add in your vanilla until combined. Fold in your whipped topping. Spread the topping over the cooled bars, then top with diced strawberries.

MISSISSIPPI MUD BARS

Chocolate and marshmallow? How could you go wrong with that combination? These rich fudge bars are topped with marshmallows and frosted with a poured chocolate frosting. Ooey, gooey and delicious, these are a potluck hit!

MAKES 12 TO 15

1 cup (240 g) unsalted butter

⅔ cup (85 g) cocoa powder

1 cup (200 g) granulated sugar

1 cup (180 g) brown sugar

4 eggs

1½ tsp (8 ml) vanilla extract

1 cup (120 g) all-purpose flour

½ tsp salt

½ tsp baking powder

4 cups (200 g) mini marshmallows

FROSTING

7 tbsp (105 g) unsalted butter, softened

2 tbsp (30 g) unsweetened cocoa powder

3 tbsp (45 ml) milk

1 tsp vanilla extract

2 cups (200 g) powdered sugar

Preheat the oven to 350°F (177°C, or gas mark 4). Line a 9 x 13–inch (23 x 33–cm) pan with nonstick cooking spray. Set aside.

Add the butter to a microwave-safe dish. Melt in the microwave, about 1 minute. Remove from the microwave, then stir in your cocoa powder. Whisk in both your sugars. Whisk in your eggs one at a time, making sure to fully incorporate after each addition. Add in the vanilla.

In a small bowl, mix together your flour, salt and baking powder. Then whisk it into the chocolate mixture. Spread into the prepared pan, and bake for 35 minutes or until the center is set. Remove the bars from the oven, and spread your marshmallows over the top. Return to the oven to bake 4 minutes longer until the marshmallows are just puffy. Remove the bars from the oven, and set aside.

To make the frosting, in a medium saucepan over medium-high heat, add your butter, cocoa powder, milk and vanilla and heat until melted. Remove from the heat, and stir in your powdered sugar. Immediately pour the frosting over the bars, then let sit for 30 minutes to let the frosting set.

MUDDY BUDDY BROWNIES

If you love the traditional snack, these brownies are even better. A moist and flavorful brownie
is topped with a thick peanut butter filling, and then sprinkled with powdered sugar.
You get all the flavors of the classic treat times ten!

—————————————————— MAKES 12 TO 16 ——————————————————

1 cup (240 g) unsalted butter

⅔ cup (85 g) unsweetened cocoa powder

1 cup (200 g) granulated sugar

1 cup (180 g) brown sugar

4 eggs

1½ tsp (8 ml) vanilla extract

1 cup (120 g) all-purpose flour

½ tsp salt

½ tsp baking powder

PEANUT BUTTER LAYER

1 cup (240 g) unsalted butter, melted

2 cups (180 g) graham cracker crumbs

¼ cup (45 g) brown sugar

1¾ cups (175 g) powdered sugar

1 cup (180 g) peanut butter

½ tsp vanilla extract

Powdered sugar, for garnish

Preheat the oven to 350°F (177°C, or gas mark 4). Line a 9 x 13-inch (23 x 33-cm) pan with nonstick cooking spray. Set aside.

Add the butter to a microwave-safe dish. Melt the butter in the microwave, about 1 minute. Remove from the microwave, then stir in your cocoa powder and whisk in both your sugars. Whisk in your eggs one at a time, making sure to fully incorporate after each addition then add in your vanilla.

In a small bowl, mix together your flour, salt and baking powder. Then whisk it into the chocolate mixture. Spread into the prepared pan, and bake for 35 minutes or until the center is set. Remove the brownies from the oven, and let cool.

For the peanut butter layer, mix together all your peanut butter layer ingredients. Spread the mixture over the cooled brownies, cover and refrigerate until the peanut butter is set. Remove the brownies from the refrigerator, and sprinkle with the powdered sugar.

BANANA SPLIT BLONDIES

Banana splits are one summertime dessert that we can't pass up, but sometimes they can get messy. When you turn them into bars, then it really takes you to a whole other level. A banana blondie is topped with a delicious pineapple buttercream and covered in peanuts, hot fudge, whipped topping and cherries!

———— MAKES 12 ————

1 cup (240 g) unsalted butter, melted

2 cups (360 g) brown sugar

2 eggs

3 tsp (15 ml) vanilla extract

2 large bananas, mashed

1 cup (120 g) all-purpose flour

1½ tsp (8 g) salt

FROSTING

1 cup (240 g) unsalted butter, softened

1 (8-oz [227-g]) can crushed pineapple, drained

6-7 cups (600-700 g) powdered sugar

Hot fudge, for garnish

Chopped peanuts, for garnish

Whipped topping, for garnish

Maraschino cherries, for garnish

Preheat the oven to 350°F (177°C, or gas mark 4). Spray a 9 x 13-inch (23 x 33-cm) pan with nonstick cooking spray. Set aside.

In a stand mixer, beat together your melted butter and brown sugar until combined. Add in your eggs and vanilla, and beat until mixed. Add in your bananas and mix until blended well. Slowly add your flour and salt, and mix until it just comes together. Spread into the prepared pan, and bake for 35 to 40 minutes or until slightly golden. Remove the blondies from the oven, and set aside to cool completely.

To make the frosting, in a stand mixer, beat together your butter and pineapple until combined. Add in your powdered sugar 1 cup (100 g) at a time until you reach your desired consistency.

Spread the frosting over the cooled blondies. Drizzle with hot fudge sauce, and sprinkle with peanuts. Add your whipped topping to a piping bag fitted with an open star tip, pipe 12 swirls over the top and place a cherry on each.

BLUEBERRY PIE BARS

These bars are a cross between pie, muffins and bars! They have all the delicious tasty flavors of each rolled into one handheld treat! This is perfect for the morning, afternoon or night!

─────────────── MAKES 9 ───────────────

CRUST

1½ cups (180 g) all-purpose flour

½ tsp baking powder

½ cup (100 g) granulated sugar

½ cup (120 g) unsalted butter, softened

½ tsp almond extract

1 egg

FILLING

2 cups (200 g) fresh blueberries

¼ cup (50 g) granulated sugar

2 tsp (6 g) cornstarch

1 tbsp (15 ml) lemon juice

Preheat the oven to 375°F (190°C, or gas mark 5). Spray an 8 x 8-inch (20 x 20-cm) baking pan with nonstick cooking spray. Set aside.

In a large bowl, add your flour, baking powder, sugar, butter, almond extract and egg. Beat with a hand mixer until the dough is crumbly. Press half of your dough into the bottom of the pan. Set aside.

To make the filling, in a bowl, toss together the blueberries, sugar, cornstarch and lemon juice until coated. Pour the mixture over your prepared crust, then sprinkle the remaining dough pieces over top of the blueberry filling. Bake in the oven for 40 minutes until the juices from the blueberries are bubbling and the crumbs are golden.

Remove the bars from the oven, and let them cool completely before serving.

CHOCOLATE CHIP GOOEY BUTTER BARS

If you've never had gooey butter cake, you're missing out! This chocolate chip version is utterly delicious. It has a cake-like bottom filled with a cream cheese center and sweet chocolate chips! It's sprinkled with powdered sugar and drizzled in melted chocolate.

―――――――――――― MAKES 12 TO 15 ――――――――――――

CRUST

1 (15.25-oz [432-g]) box yellow cake mix

½ cup (120 g) unsalted butter, melted

1 egg

1 cup (175 g) semi-sweet chocolate chips

FILLING

1 (8-oz [320-g]) package cream cheese, softened

2 eggs

1 tsp vanilla extract

3 cups (300 g) powdered sugar, plus extra for topping

TOPPING

¼ cup (45 g) semi-sweet chocolate chips

½ tsp vegetable oil

Preheat the oven to 325°F (163°C, or gas mark 3). Spray a 9 x 13–inch (23 x 33–cm) baking pan with nonstick cooking spray. Set aside.

In a large bowl, mix together the cake mix, butter and egg with a hand mixer until combined. Fold in the chocolate chips. Press the mixture into the bottom of the prepared pan. Set aside.

In another bowl, beat together your cream cheese, eggs and vanilla until smooth. Add in your powdered sugar 1 cup (100 g) at a time until combined.

Pour the filling over the crust. Bake for 40 to 45 minutes until the center is just set. Remove the bars from the oven, and let cool. Once cooled, sprinkle with extra powdered sugar.

To make the topping, add the chocolate chips and oil to a microwave-safe bowl and melt. Drizzle it over the powdered sugar.

BETTER-THAN-SEX BROWNIES

If you're a fan of the cake, then you'll love the brownie version. A fudge brownie is poked and poured with delicious caramel. It is then frosted with vanilla buttercream and topped with toffee bits, making these bars a delicious alternative.

───────── MAKES 12 TO 16 ─────────

1 cup (240 g) unsalted butter

⅔ cup (85 g) unsweetened cocoa powder

1 cup (200 g) granulated sugar

1 cup (180 g) brown sugar

4 eggs

1½ tsp (8 ml) vanilla extract

1 cup (120 g) all-purpose flour

½ tsp salt

½ tsp baking powder

½ cup (120 ml) caramel sauce

FROSTING

1 cup (240 g) unsalted butter, softened

2 tsp (10 ml) vanilla extract

4 cups (400 g) powdered sugar

½ cup (75 g) toffee bits, for garnish

Preheat the oven to 350°F (177°C, or gas mark 4). Line a 9 x 13–inch (23 x 33–cm) pan with nonstick cooking spray. Set aside.

Add the butter to a microwave-safe bowl. Melt the butter in the microwave, about 1 minute. Remove from the microwave, then stir in your cocoa powder. Whisk in both your sugars until combined. Whisk in your eggs one at a time, making sure to fully incorporate well after each addition. Add in the vanilla.

In a small bowl, mix together your flour, salt and baking powder. Then whisk it into your chocolate mixture. Spread into the prepared pan, and bake for 35 minutes or until the center is set. Remove the brownies from the oven and let cool. Once cooled, poke holes over the top of the brownies with a wooden skewer. Pour the caramel sauce over the top, and spread it into the holes with a spatula. Place the cake in the refrigerator to set, about 1 hour.

To make the frosting, beat your butter with a hand mixer until light and fluffy, then add in your vanilla until blended. Add in your powdered sugar 1 cup (100 g) at a time until the desired consistency is reached. Spread the frosting over the cooled brownies, and top with toffee bits.

SALTED NUT ROLL BARS

This recipe has been in our family for years. We love the salted nut roll, but who could ever just stop at one? How about turning them into bars so you have a pan full of the delicious candy bar favorite. Quick and easy to whip up, and enough to feed a crowd.

— MAKES 12 TO 16 —

1 (16-oz [454-g]) container salted dry roasted peanuts, divided

4 tbsp (60 g) unsalted butter

1 (14-oz [396-g]) can sweetened condensed milk

1 (10-oz [283-g]) bag peanut butter chips

4 cups (200 g) mini marshmallows

Spray a 9 x 13–inch (23 x 33–cm) baking pan with nonstick cooking spray. Spread half of your container of peanuts into the bottom of the prepared pan. Set aside.

In a large saucepan on the stove, add your butter and melt on medium-high heat, about 1 to 2 minutes. Once melted, add your sweetened condensed milk and stir until combined. Add in your peanut butter chips, and stir until melted and creamy. Fold in your mini marshmallows and cook just until they are puffy.

Remove the saucepan from the heat, and immediately spread the mixture into the pan on top of your peanuts. Top with the remaining peanuts, and press them down into the top gently. Refrigerate for about 1 hour until set.

FLUFFERNUTTER BARS

Fluffernutter sandwiches were a kid favorite when I was growing up. So, it was logical to make them into bar form! A peanut butter bar is topped with a marshmallow buttercream and covered with chopped peanuts.

──────────────── MAKES 12 TO 15 ────────────────

¾ cup (180 g) unsalted butter, melted

1 cup (180 g) brown sugar

½ cup (100 g) granulated sugar

2 eggs

2 tsp (10 ml) vanilla extract

¾ cup (135 g) creamy peanut butter

½ tsp salt

1½ cup (180 g) all-purpose flour

FROSTING

½ cup (120 g) unsalted butter, softened

1 (7-oz [198-g]) container marshmallow fluff

2 cups (200 g) powdered sugar

½ cup (75 g) chopped peanuts

Preheat the oven to 350°F (177°C, or gas mark 4). Grease a 9 x 13–inch (23 x 33–cm) pan with nonstick cooking spray. Set aside.

In a large bowl, mix together the butter, brown sugar and granulated sugar with a hand mixer until blended. Add in your eggs and vanilla extract until incorporated. Add in your peanut butter, and continue to beat until combined.

In a bowl, whisk together the salt and flour. Slowly add to your wet mixture and mix until just combined.

Spread into the prepared pan. Bake for 25 to 30 minutes until golden and a toothpick inserted in the center comes out clean. Remove the bars from the oven and let cool completely.

To make the frosting, in large bowl, beat together the butter and marshmallow fluff. Add in your powdered sugar 1 cup (100 g) at a time until blended.

Spread the frosting on the bars, and sprinkle peanuts on top.

LEMON MERINGUE PIE BARS

Growing up, there was never a family function where one of my relatives *didn't* bring over a gigantic lemon meringue pie. Well, how about switching it up and making it into a delicious bar? A shortbread crust is topped with a delicious lemon filling and covered in a meringue topping. Truly a fun twist on the classic treat.

———————————— MAKES 12 TO 16 ————————————

CRUST

1 cup (240 g) unsalted butter, softened

2 cups (240 g) all-purpose flour

½ cup (100 g) granulated sugar

¼ tsp salt

FILLING

6 eggs

1¼ cups (250 g) granulated sugar

¾ cup (90 g) all-purpose flour

¼ tsp salt

¾ cup (180 ml) fresh lemon juice

TOPPING

4 egg whites

½ cup (100 g) granulated sugar

Preheat the oven to 350°F (177°C, or gas mark 4). Line a 9 x 13-inch (23 x 33-cm) pan with parchment paper. Set aside.

In a food processor, add your butter, flour, sugar and salt. Process until crumbs form, then dump out on the prepared pan and press down to form crust. Bake for 20 to 22 minutes until the edges are golden. Remove from the oven. Set aside.

To make the filling, whisk together your eggs and sugar until combined, then stir in your flour and salt until incorporated. Stir in the lemon juice. Pour the filling into the hot crust, then return it to the oven. Bake for 20 minutes until the center is just set.

To make the topping, in a stand mixer fitted with a whisk attachment, add your egg whites and sugar. Beat on high until stiff peaks form, about 3 to 4 minutes.

Spread the topping over the filling layer and swirl around to create peaks. Bake for 8 to 10 minutes until just starting to brown on top. Remove the bars from the oven, and let cool completely.

INVENTIVE

COOKIES

Who else grew up with Grandma sugaring you up with
her fresh baked cookies? I know I did. In this chapter, you
will find a multitude of flavor options from Peach Cobbler
Cookies (page 126) to Fluffernutter Cookies (page 104).
Whatever your age, this chapter is for you!

FLUFFERNUTTER COOKIES

My kids are obsessed with fluffernutter sandwiches, and I've always loved to bake with the peanut butter and marshmallow flavors together. These peanut butter cookies sandwich a light and fluffy marshmallow filling. It takes great strength to not eat a whole batch!

————————————— MAKES 12 —————————————

½ cup (120 g) unsalted butter, softened

½ cup (68 g) peanut butter

½ cup (100 g) granulated sugar

½ cup (90 g) brown sugar

1 egg

1 tsp vanilla extract

1¼ cups (150 g) all-purpose flour

1 tsp baking soda

¼ tsp salt

FILLING

½ cup (120 g) unsalted butter, softened

1½ cups (150 g) powdered sugar

1 tsp vanilla extract

1 (7-oz [198-g]) container marshmallow fluff

Preheat the oven to 350°F (177°C, or gas mark 4). Line a cookie sheet with parchment paper. Set aside.

In a large bowl, cream together your butter, peanut butter, granulated sugar and brown sugar with a hand mixer until smooth. Add in your egg and vanilla, and beat until blended. Add in your flour, baking soda and salt, and mix until just combined.

Using a medium cookie scoop, scoop the dough out and roll it into balls. Place them on the prepared baking sheet 2 inches (5 cm) apart.

Bake for 10 to 15 minutes until the edges are starting to just brown. Remove the cookies from the oven, and let them cool on the pan for a few minutes before transferring to a cooling rack to cool completely. Repeat with the remaining dough.

To make the filling, in a stand mixer, beat together your butter and powdered sugar until smooth. Add in your vanilla and marshmallow fluff until blended.

Once the cookies are cool, add your filling mixture to a piping bag and cut the tip off. Flip the cookies over to expose the flat side, pipe the filling over the cookie and top with another cookie. Repeat with each cookie.

PIÑA COLADA COOKIES

How about having a favorite fruity drink in cookie form? That's a big yes from me! These Piña Colada Cookies are filled with all the flavor of the cocktail! Pineapple, coconut, rum and cherries. It's a tasty cookie, and you can't stop at just one.

MAKES 30 TO 36

1 cup (240 g) unsalted butter, softened

1 cup (180 g) brown sugar

1 cup (200 g) granulated sugar

2 eggs

1 (8-oz [227-g]) can crushed pineapple, drained

1 tsp vanilla extract

½ tsp coconut extract

4 cups (480 g) all-purpose flour

2 tsp (7 g) baking powder

1 tsp baking soda

¼ tsp salt

1 cup (75 g) shredded sweetened coconut

1 cup (95 g) maraschino cherries, diced

RUM GLAZE

1 cup (100 g) powdered sugar

1 tsp rum extract

Preheat the oven to 350°F (177°C, or gas mark 4). Line a cookie sheet with parchment paper. Set aside.

In a stand mixer, cream together your butter, brown sugar and granulated sugar until combined. Add in your eggs, pineapple, vanilla and coconut extract, and mix until incorporated.

In another large bowl, whisk together your flour, baking powder, baking soda and salt. Slowly add your dry ingredients into your wet ingredients. Turn the mixer to low and add in your coconut and cherries until combined.

Drop the dough by tablespoons (15 g) about 2 inches (5 cm) apart onto the prepared baking sheet. Bake for 12 to 15 minutes until the edges are just turning golden. Remove the cookies from the oven, and place them on a cooling rack to cool. Repeat with the remaining dough.

To make the glaze, whisk together your powdered sugar and rum extract, and drizzle over the cooled cookies. Let the glaze set for about 10 minutes.

ROCKY ROAD COOKIES

One of our favorite ice cream flavors is rocky road. It has so much in one little portion that the flavors are hard to pass up! These cookies combine chocolate, marshmallow and peanuts all into one handheld treat!

—————————————————— MAKES 24 ——————————————————

2 cups (240 g) all-purpose flour

½ cup (50 g) unsweetened cocoa powder

1 tsp baking powder

½ tsp salt

¾ cup (180 g) unsalted butter, softened

¾ cup (135 g) brown sugar

1 cup (200 g) granulated sugar

2 eggs

1 tsp vanilla extract

1 cup (150 g) peanuts

1½ cups (75 g) mini marshmallows

Preheat your oven to 350°F (177°C, or gas mark 4). Line a cookie sheet with parchment paper. Set aside.

In a medium bowl, whisk together your flour, cocoa powder, baking powder and salt.

In a stand mixer cream together your butter, brown sugar and granulated sugar until light and fluffy. Add in your eggs and vanilla, and beat until combined. Add in your dry ingredients and mix until incorporated, then fold in your peanuts and marshmallows.

Scoop dough by tablespoonfuls (15 g) onto the prepared baking sheet about 2 inches (5 cm) apart. Bake for 10 minutes, then remove from the oven. Let cool for 5 minutes on the baking sheet before transferring to a cooling rack to cool completely.

LEMON POPPYSEED COOKIES

When spring rolls around, lemon is a flavor that I can't ignore. Lemon poppyseed bread
has long been a favorite in our family, but these cookies are even better! They make a ton,
and the whole family will be asking for more!

MAKES 36

1 cup (240 g) unsalted butter, softened

2 cups (400 g) granulated sugar

Zest of 1 large lemon

3 tbsp (45 ml) lemon juice

2 eggs

1 tsp vanilla extract

2 tsp (10 g) baking soda

½ tsp baking powder

3½ cups (240 g) all-purpose flour

½ tsp salt

1 tbsp (15 g) poppyseeds

In a stand mixer, beat together your butter and sugar until light and fluffy. Add in your lemon zest and lemon juice, and mix until combined. Add in your eggs and vanilla, and beat until incorporated.

In a large bowl, mix together your baking soda, baking powder, flour and salt. Slowly add this mixture into your wet ingredients. Lastly, mix in your poppyseeds. Cover and refrigerate for 1 hour.

While the dough is chilling, preheat your oven to 350°F (177°C, or gas mark 4). Line a baking sheet with parchment paper. Set aside. Once the dough is chilled, take about 2 tablespoons (30 g) of dough into your hand and roll it into a ball. Place the dough balls 2 inches (5 cm) apart on the baking sheet.

Bake for 10 to 12 minutes or until the edges are just turning golden. Remove the cookies from the oven, and let them cool for 5 minutes on the baking sheet before transferring to a cooling rack to cool completely.

BANANA CREAM COOKIES

Banana cream anything is high on my list of favorite desserts. These cookies encompass everything that I love! A soft and fluffy banana-flavored cookie is frosted with a creamy white frosting that you cannot get enough of!

— MAKES 20 —

½ cup (120 g) unsalted butter, softened

1 cup (200 g) granulated sugar

½ cup (60 g) sour cream

2 eggs

½ tsp vanilla extract

3 cups (360 g) all-purpose flour

1½ tsp (6 g) baking powder

½ tsp baking soda

½ tsp salt

1 (3.4-oz [96-g]) package banana pudding

FROSTING

½ cup (120 g) unsalted butter, softened

1 (8-oz [230-g]) package cream cheese, softened

4 cups (400 g) powdered sugar

1 tsp vanilla extract

Sliced banana, for garnish (optional)

Preheat the oven to 350°F (177°C, or gas mark 4). Line a baking sheet with parchment paper. Set aside.

In a stand mixer, beat together your butter, sugar, sour cream, eggs and vanilla until smooth.

In a medium bowl, whisk together your flour, baking powder, baking soda, salt and pudding. With a mixer on low, slowly add in your dry ingredients until combined.

Take about 2 tablespoons (30 g) of your dough and roll it into a ball and place it on the baking sheet. Press the dough flat gently with the palm of your hand.

Bake in the oven for 12 to 15 minutes until slightly golden. Remove the cookies from the oven, and place them on a cooling rack to cool completely.

To make the frosting, in a stand mixer, beat together your butter and cream cheese until smooth. Add in your powdered sugar 1 cup (100 g) at a time until combined, then mix in your vanilla. Spread about 2 tablespoons (30 g) onto each cookie and top with slices of banana, if desired.

STRAWBERRIES-AND-CREAM COOKIES

When the weather gets warm, we love to have strawberries and cream on hand.
These cookies are a handheld version of that! A moist and chewy cookie is stuffed full of
strawberries and white chocolate chips, giving you a flavor explosion with each bite.

MAKES 16 TO 18

2¼ cups (270 g) all-purpose flour

1 tsp baking soda

½ tsp salt

¾ cup (180 g) unsalted butter, softened

½ cup (100 g) granulated sugar

½ cup (90 g) brown sugar

1 tbsp (15 ml) vanilla extract

2 eggs

1 cup (175 g) white chocolate chips

¾ cup (150 g) diced strawberries

Preheat the oven to 350°F (177°C, or gas mark 4). Line a baking sheet with parchment paper or a Silpat mat. Set aside.

In a bowl, whisk together your flour, baking soda and salt. Set aside.

In a stand mixer, beat together your butter, granulated sugar and brown sugar until light and fluffy. Add in your vanilla and eggs until blended. Slowly add in your dry ingredients until combined. Fold in your chocolate chips and strawberries.

Grab about 2 tablespoons (30 g) of dough and roll it into a ball and place on the prepared cookie sheet about 2 inches (5 cm) apart. Bake for 10 to 12 minutes or until slightly golden. Remove the cookies from the oven, and let them cool on the pan for 5 minutes before transferring to a wire rack to cool completely. Repeat with the remaining dough.

CINNAMON ROLL COOKIES

Breakfast for dessert? Don't mind if I do! These Cinnamon Roll Cookies take one of your favorite breakfast treats and turn it into a crunchy and deliciously spiced cookie that you can't help but love.

MAKES 30

2 cups (120 g) all-purpose flour

½ tsp baking powder

½ tsp salt

¾ cup (180 g) unsalted butter, softened

½ cup (100 g) granulated sugar

¼ cup (45 g) brown sugar

1 egg

1½ tsp (8 ml) vanilla extract

FILLING

4 tbsp (60 g) unsalted butter, very soft

½ cup (90 g) brown sugar

1 tsp cinnamon

GLAZE

½ cup (50 g) powdered sugar

2 tbsp (30 ml) heavy cream

½ tsp vanilla extract

In a bowl, whisk together your flour, baking powder and salt. Set aside. In a stand mixer beat together your butter, granulated sugar and brown sugar until fluffy. Add in your egg and vanilla until blended. Slowly add in your dry ingredients and mix until it comes together. Remove the dough from the mixer and form it into a disc. Wrap it in plastic wrap, and refrigerate for 1 hour.

While the dough is chilling, preheat your oven to 350°F (177°C, or gas mark 4). Line a baking sheet with parchment paper. Set aside. Make your filling by adding all your ingredients to a bowl and mixing until it all comes together.

Unwrap your cookie dough and split it into two. Roll each portion out on a lightly-floured surface into about a 10 x 8-inch (25 x 20-cm) rectangle and ¼ inch (6 mm) thick. Spread half of your filling mixture over the dough, leaving about a 1-inch (2.5-cm) edge from all sides. Tightly roll your dough, up from the long end to create a log. Trim off the edges. Cut into 15 equal pieces about ½ inch (13 mm) wide.

Place the cookies on the baking sheet, and bake for about 22 minutes until slightly golden.

Remove the cookies from the oven, and let them cool on the cookie sheet for about 5 minutes before transferring to a wire rack to cool completely. Repeat with the remaining dough.

To make the glaze, add your ingredients to a small bowl, and whisk together.

Drizzle over the top of the cooled cookies.

S'MORES COOKIES

Hello, bonfire favorite! Who doesn't love the classic graham cracker, chocolate marshmallow treat? These cookies have crushed up graham crackers baked right in, big chunks of chocolate and gooey marshmallows.

MAKES 24

1 cup (240 g) unsalted butter, softened

¾ cup (135 g) brown sugar

¾ cup (150 g) granulated sugar

2 eggs

2 tbsp (30 ml) vanilla extract

¾ tsp baking soda

¾ tsp salt

1½ cups (180 g) all-purpose flour

1½ cups (135 g) graham cracker crumbs

1 (12-oz [340-g]) bag semi-sweet chocolate chunks

1½ cups (75 g) mini marshmallows

Preheat the oven to 350°F (177°C, or gas mark 4).

In a stand mixer, beat together your butter, brown sugar and granulated sugar until light and fluffy. Add in your eggs and vanilla, and mix until combined.

In a medium bowl, whisk together your baking soda, salt, flour and graham cracker crumbs. Slowly add the dry ingredients into the wet and mix until combined. Add in your chocolate chunks until combined.

Drop the dough by rounded tablespoonfuls (15 g) onto an ungreased cookie sheet. Bake for 10 minutes or until the edges are slightly golden. Remove the cookies from the oven, and press 3 to 4 marshmallows into the tops of the cookies. Transfer to a cooling rack to cool completely.

BIRTHDAY CAKE COOKIES

Who doesn't love cake and cookies? With these Birthday Cake Cookies, you have the best of both worlds! A chewy funfetti cookie is frosted with a fun colorful buttercream frosting and garnished with sprinkles—making these cookies even better than the cake!

MAKES 12 TO 15

1 (15.25-oz [432-g]) box funfetti cake mix

2 eggs

⅓ cup (80 ml) vegetable oil

½ cup (80 g) rainbow sprinkles

1 tsp vanilla extract

FROSTING

1 cup (240 g) unsalted butter, softened

1 tsp vanilla extract

½ tsp almond extract

3–4 cups (300–400 g) powdered sugar

Pink food coloring

Rainbow sprinkles, for garnish (optional)

Preheat the oven to 350°F (177°C, or gas mark 4). Line a baking sheet with parchment paper. Set aside.

In a large bowl, mix together your cake mix, eggs, vegetable oil, sprinkles and vanilla with a hand mixer. Grab about 2 tablespoons (30 g) of dough, roll it into a ball and place it on the baking sheet. With a drinking glass, gently press the balls down until about ¼ inch (6 mm) thick. Bake for 12 to 14 minutes until the edges are slightly golden. Remove the cookies from the oven, and cool them on the pan for about 5 minutes before transferring to a cooling rack to cool completely.

To make the frosting, with a hand mixer, beat your butter until light and fluffy, then add in your vanilla and almond extracts until incorporated. Adding 1 cup (100 g) at a time, mix in your powdered sugar until the desired consistency is reached. Lastly, add in a few drops of pink food coloring to reach your desired color. Add your frosting to a piping bag fitted with a star tip, and swirl frosting over the cooled cookies. Sprinkle with the rainbow sprinkles, if desired.

SCOTCHEROO COOKIES

One of my favorite treats growing up were my mom's scotcheroos! They were the go-to bar that everyone wanted. These cookies are those bars in smaller portions. Quick, easy and delicious. They whip up fast, use minimal ingredients and the kids love them!

MAKES 24 TO 30

6 cups (150 g) puffed rice cereal

½ cup (120 g) unsalted butter

2 cups (400 g) granulated sugar

½ cup (120 ml) milk

4 tbsp (30 g) cocoa powder

1 tsp salt

½ cup (90 g) butterscotch chips

2 tsp (10 ml) vanilla extract

In a large bowl, add your puffed rice cereal. Set aside. Line your countertop with parchment paper.

In a large pot on the stove, add your butter, sugar, milk, cocoa powder, salt and butterscotch chips. Bring to a boil and let boil for 1 minute, or until the butterscotch chips are melted. Remove from the heat, and stir in your vanilla. Pour over your puffed rice cereal, and mix until combined and all the cereal is coated.

Using a medium cookie scoop, drop by dollops onto parchment paper. Let cool for 30 minutes.

TIRAMISU COOKIES

I would be lying if I said I didn't enjoy a little coffee in my dessert. These Tiramisu Cookies are a chewy, coffee-flavored cookie with a creamy mascarpone frosting that makes them almost better than the original.

—————————————— MAKES 20 TO 24 ——————————————

½ cup (120 g) unsalted butter, melted

½ cup (100 g) granulated sugar

½ cup (90 g) brown sugar

1 egg

1 tbsp (3 g) instant coffee granules

2 tsp (10 ml) vanilla extract

½ tsp baking powder

1½ cups (180 g) all-purpose flour

FROSTING

½ cup (120 g) unsalted butter, softened

½ cup (115 g) mascarpone cheese, softened

2 tbsp (6 g) instant coffee granules

3 tsp (15 ml) water

4 cups (400 g) powdered sugar

2–4 tbsp (30–60 ml) milk, if desired

1 tbsp (15 g) unsweetened cocoa powder

Preheat your oven to 350°F (177°C, or gas mark 4). Lightly grease a cookie sheet with nonstick cooking spray. Set aside.

In a stand mixer, mix together your butter, granulated sugar and brown sugar until combined. Add in your egg, coffee granules and vanilla, and beat until incorporated.

In another bowl, whisk together your baking powder and flour. Slowly add it to your wet ingredients. Roll the dough into 1- to 1½-inch (2.5- to 3.8-cm) balls and place them 2 inches (5 cm) apart on the prepared cookie sheet. Using a small cup dipped in some sugar, gently press down slightly until they are about 2 inches (5 cm) wide. Bake for 12 to 15 minutes until the edges are golden but the center is still soft. Remove the cookies from the oven, and let them cool on a cookie sheet for 5 minutes before transferring to a wire rack to cool completely. Repeat with the remaining dough.

To make the frosting, in a stand mixer, beat together your butter and mascarpone cheese until smooth. In a small bowl, dissolve your coffee granules in water. Add it to your butter-and-cheese mixture and mix until blended. Add in your powdered sugar 1 cup (100 g) at a time. Add milk 1 tablespoon (15 ml) at a time until you reach your desired consistency.

Add the frosting to a piping bag fitted with an open star tip, and pipe swirls over the tops of the cooled cookies. Sprinkle with cocoa powder.

FRUIT TART COOKIES

We love fruit tarts around this house, but sometimes they can become a little much for one person to eat. Welcome these fruit tart cookies: a scaled down, soft and delicious version of the classic tart. Topped with various fruits and a creamy frosting, these are fresh, light and delicious.

MAKES 12

½ cup (120 g) unsalted butter, softened

⅔ cup (130 g) granulated sugar

1 egg

½ tsp vanilla extract

½ tsp almond extract

1¼ cups (150 g) all-purpose flour

½ tsp baking powder

¼ tsp salt

FROSTING

1 (8-oz [230-g]) package cream cheese, softened

2 tbsp (30 g) butter, softened

½ tsp vanilla extract

½ tsp almond extract

2 cups (200 g) powdered sugar

Strawberries, sliced

Kiwi, sliced

Blueberries

Preheat the oven to 350°F (177°C, or gas mark 4). Line a baking sheet with parchment paper. Set aside.

In a stand mixer, beat together your butter and sugar. Add in the egg, vanilla and almond extract until incorporated.

In a bowl, whisk together your flour, baking powder and salt. Slowly add the flour mixture into your butter mixture until combined.

Roll into 2-inch (5-cm) balls and place on the baking sheet 2 inches (5 cm) apart. Gently press down with your palm to flatten slightly, and bake for 10 to 12 minutes until just golden. Remove the cookies from the oven, and let them cool on the baking sheet for 5 minutes before transferring to a wire rack to cool completely.

To make the frosting, in a bowl, beat together the cream cheese and butter with a hand mixer until combined and smooth. Add in your vanilla and almond extracts until incorporated. Mix in your powdered sugar 1 cup (100 g) at a time until blended. Spread the frosting thick over the tops of the cooled cookies, and top with fruit.

PEACH COBBLER COOKIES

I've never had a peach cobbler that I didn't love. But I have a hard time holding back from eating the whole pan. These Peach Cobbler Cookies are little individual cobblers that are fun, easy and seriously tasty!

MAKES 20 TO 24

1 cup (240 g) unsalted butter, softened

¾ cup (150 g) granulated sugar

½ cup (90 g) brown sugar

1 egg

1 egg yolk

2 tsp (10 ml) vanilla extract

3 cups (360 g) all-purpose flour

1 tsp baking powder

1½ tsp (8 g) cream of tartar

1 tsp salt

1½ tsp (4 g) cinnamon

1 cup (225 g) diced peaches (canned or fresh—if canned, drain first!)

ROLLING

½ cup (50 g) granulated sugar

1 tbsp (8 g) cinnamon

Preheat the oven to 325°F (163°C, or gas mark 3). Line a baking sheet with parchment paper or a Silpat mat. Set aside.

In a stand mixer, beat together your butter, granulated sugar and brown sugar until light and fluffy. Add in the egg, egg yolk and vanilla, and beat until incorporated.

In another bowl, whisk together your flour, baking powder, cream of tartar, salt and cinnamon. With a mixer on low, slowly add in your flour mixture until combined. Gently fold in the peaches.

In a small bowl, whisk together your sugar and cinnamon. Set aside.

Scoop 2 tablespoons (30 g) of dough and roll it into a ball. Roll balls into your cinnamon and sugar mixture, and place them on the prepared baking sheet about 2 inches (5 cm) apart. Bake for 10 to 12 minutes until slightly golden. Remove the cookies from the oven, and let them cool on the baking sheet for 5 minutes before transferring to a wire rack to cool completely.

CHOCOLATE PEANUT BUTTER CORNFLAKE COOKIES

Cornflake cookies are where it's at. If you want a simple cookie with huge flavor, then these are it! They take little time and few ingredients to make, and drizzling them with a little chocolate makes them just that much more irresistible.

———————————————— MAKES 24 ————————————————

6 cups (150 g) cornflake cereal

1 cup (240 ml) corn syrup

1 cup (200 g) granulated sugar

1 cup (180 g) peanut butter

¼ cup (45 g) semi-sweet chocolate chips

½ tsp vegetable oil

Line your countertop with parchment paper. Add your cornflakes to a large bowl. Set aside.

In a medium saucepan over medium heat, stir together the corn syrup and sugar until the sugar dissolves, about 3 to 4 minutes. Do not bring to a boil.

Once dissolved, remove from the heat and stir in your peanut butter until smooth.

Pour over the cornflakes, and gently stir together until all the cereal is coated.

Drop the mixture by heaping tablespoonfuls (15 g) onto the parchment paper, and let cool 30 minutes.

In a small microwave-safe bowl, add together your chocolate chips and vegetable oil. Heat in the microwave for about 1 minute, stirring every 30 seconds until melted, then drizzle over the cookies. Let sit for 15 minutes to set up before serving.

CAPTIVATING
CUPCAKES

Someone once told me that cupcakes were the king of all desserts, that they are personalized individual cakes just for you. I'm starting to agree. From Pancake Cupcakes (page 137) to Chocolate-Covered Strawberry Cupcakes (page 154) this is a chapter full of fun, easy and approachable treats that will have you loving these handheld goodies!

ALMOND JOY CUPCAKES

I love candy bars. Almond Joys have been one that my mom has had in the cupboard since I was a kid. These Almond Joy Cupcakes are a chocolate cupcake filled with a creamy coconut filling and topped with a light and fluffy almond buttercream. They have all the flavors of the family-favorite candy!

MAKES 12 TO 14

1 cup (120 g) all-purpose flour

1 cup (200 g) granulated sugar

½ cup (50 g) unsweetened cocoa powder

1 tsp baking powder

½ tsp baking soda

½ tsp salt

1 tsp vanilla extract

2 eggs

½ cup (120 ml) milk

½ cup (120 ml) water

¼ cup (60 ml) vegetable oil

FILLING

3 cups (300 g) sweetened shredded coconut

1 (14-oz [396-g]) can sweetened condensed milk

FROSTING

1 cup (240 g) unsalted butter, softened

4 cups (400 g) powdered sugar

2 tsp (5 ml) almond extract

½ tsp vanilla extract

Shredded coconut, for garnish

Whole almonds, for garnish (optional)

Preheat the oven to 350°F (177°C, or gas mark 4). Line a 12-count cupcake pan with liners. Set aside.

In a stand mixer, add your flour, sugar, cocoa powder, baking powder, baking soda and salt. Mix together until blended, then add in your vanilla and eggs. Add in your milk, water and oil one at a time, mixing well after each addition.

Fill your cupcake liners two-thirds full with batter. Bake for 18 to 20 minutes until a toothpick inserted in the center comes out clean and the tops of the cupcakes spring back when touched. Remove from the oven to cool.

To make the filling, stir together the coconut and sweetened condensed milk. Set aside. Using a melon baller or cupcake corer remove the center of the cupcakes and place about 1 heaping tablespoon (15 g) of your filling into the cupcakes.

To make the frosting, add your butter to a stand mixer and beat until smooth. Add in your powdered sugar 1 cup (100 g) at a time until combined. Add in your extracts until blended. Place the frosting in a large piping bag fitted with an open star tip, and pipe swirls on top of the cooled cupcakes. Sprinkle with shredded coconut and top with almonds if desired.

SWEET POTATO PIE CUPCAKES

Sweet potato pie is a favorite in our family, but so are cupcakes. So, taking one of our favorite pies and turning it into a single-serving, handheld treat was obvious. Lightly spiced and flavorfully frosted with a maple buttercream, these are a true addiction.

— MAKES 12 —

3 tbsp (43 g) unsalted butter, softened

½ cup (45 g) brown sugar

¼ cup (50 g) granulated sugar

1 egg

1 tsp vanilla

½ cup (113 g) mashed sweet potatoes

¼ cup (60 ml) vegetable oil

¼ cup (60 ml) milk

1½ cups (180 g) all-purpose flour

1 tsp cinnamon

½ tsp nutmeg

½ tsp salt

½ tbsp (6 g) baking powder

FROSTING

1 cup (240 g) unsalted butter, softened

4 cups (400 g) powdered sugar

1 tsp maple extract

2 tbsp (30 ml) milk

Toasted marshmallows, for garnish (optional)

Preheat the oven to 350°F (177°C, or gas mark 4). Line a 12-count cupcake pan with liners. Set aside.

In a stand mixer, beat together your butter, brown sugar and granulated sugar until fluffy. Add in your egg and vanilla, and beat until blended. Mix in your mashed sweet potatoes, oil and milk until smooth.

In a bowl, whisk together your flour, cinnamon, nutmeg, salt and baking powder. Slowly add it to your wet ingredients.

Fill each liner two-thirds full with batter. Bake for 18 to 20 minutes until a toothpick inserted in the center comes out clean and the tops of the cupcakes spring back when touched. Remove from the oven to cool.

To make the frosting, beat your butter in a stand mixer until smooth. Add in your powdered sugar 1 cup (100 g) at a time until you reach your desired consistency. Mix in your maple extract and milk. Add to a large piping bag fitted with an open tip, and pipe the frosting on the tops of the cooled cupcakes. Top with toasted marshmallows, if desired.

RUM-AND-COKE CUPCAKES

How about a classic bar drink as a dessert? These chocolate cupcakes are spiked with a little bit of rum and Coke, and then they are topped with a rum buttercream frosting. Give it a little twist of lime and you're set!

———————————— MAKES 12 TO 14 ————————————

1 cup (120 g) all-purpose flour

1 cup (200 g) granulated sugar

½ cup (50 g) unsweetened cocoa powder

1 tsp baking powder

½ tsp baking soda

½ tsp salt

1 tsp vanilla extract

2 eggs

1 cup (240 ml) coke

¼ cup (60 ml) rum

FROSTING

1 cup (240 g) unsalted butter, softened

4 cups (400 g) powdered sugar

2 tsp (10 ml) vanilla extract

2 tbsp (30 ml) rum

2 tbsp (30 ml) milk

Lime slices, for garnish (optional but highly recommended!)

Preheat the oven to 350°F (177°C, or gas mark 4). Line a 12-count cupcake pan with liners. Set aside.

In a stand mixer, add your flour, sugar, cocoa powder, baking powder, baking soda and salt. Mix together until blended. Add in your vanilla and eggs until combined. Add in your coke and rum, and mix until smooth.

Fill your cupcake liners two-thirds full with batter. Bake for 18 to 20 minutes until a toothpick inserted in the center comes out clean and the tops of the cupcakes spring back when touched. Remove from the oven to cool.

To make the frosting, in a stand mixer, beat your butter until smooth. Add in your powdered sugar 1 cup (100 g) at a time. Mix in your vanilla and rum, and beat until combined. Add your milk 1 tablespoon (15 ml) at a time until the desired consistency is reached. Add the frosting into a large piping bag fitted with an open star tip. Pipe swirls onto the tops of each cupcake, and top with lime slices if desired.

See image on page 130.

PANCAKE CUPCAKES

Dessert for breakfast? Don't mind if I do! These pancake cupcakes are legit pancake batter baked up in a cupcake tin. They're frosted with a 100-percent addicting maple buttercream and, to top it off, how about adding some diced bacon?

MAKES 12

1½ cups (180 g) all-purpose flour

2 tbsp (25 g) granulated sugar

1 tbsp (11 g) baking powder

1 tsp salt

1¼ cups (300 ml) buttermilk

1 egg

4 tbsp (60 g) butter, melted

1 tsp maple extract

FROSTING

1 cup (240 g) unsalted butter, softened

4 cups (400 g) powdered sugar

2 tsp (10 ml) maple extract

1–2 tbsp (15–30 ml) milk

Diced bacon, cooked, for garnish (optional)

Preheat the oven to 350°F (177°C, or gas mark 4). Line a 12-count cupcake pan with liners. Set aside.

In a large bowl, whisk together the flour, sugar, baking powder and salt. Heat the buttermilk in the microwave so it is warm to touch, about 1 to 2 minutes. Add it to the dry ingredients. Next, add in your egg, butter and maple extract. Whisk until combined, but do not overmix—lumps are okay.

Divide evenly among cupcake liners. Bake in the oven for 15 to 18 minutes until golden and the tops of the cupcakes spring back when touched. Remove from the oven, and set aside to cool.

To make the frosting, in a stand mixer, beat your butter until smooth. Add in your powdered sugar 1 cup (100 g) at a time, then add in the maple extract and milk until smooth. Add the frosting to a large piping bag fitted with an open star tip. Pipe swirls on top of the cooled cupcakes. Top with diced bacon, if desired.

ROCKY ROAD CUPCAKES

Chocolate, peanuts and marshmallows, oh my! There is nothing about these moist chocolate cupcakes that we don't love. With a light chocolate whipped frosting, this cupcake is topped with mini marshmallows, peanuts and a drizzle of chocolate syrup.

— MAKES 12 TO 14 —

1 cup (120 g) all-purpose flour

1 cup (200 g) granulated sugar

½ cup (50 g) unsweetened cocoa powder

1 tsp baking powder

½ tsp baking soda

½ tsp salt

1 tsp vanilla extract

2 eggs

½ cup (120 ml) milk

½ cup (120 ml) water

¼ cup (60 ml) vegetable oil

¼ cup (40 g) chopped peanuts

FROSTING

1 (4-oz [96-g]) package chocolate pudding

¼ cup (25 g) powdered sugar

1 cup (240 ml) milk

1 (8-oz [226-g]) container whipped topping

Chopped peanuts, for garnish

Mini marshmallows, for garnish

Chocolate syrup, for garnish

Preheat the oven to 350°F (177°C, or gas mark 4). Line a 12-count cupcake pan with liners. Set aside.

In a stand mixer, add your flour, sugar, cocoa powder, baking powder, baking soda and salt. Mix together until blended. Add in your vanilla and eggs until incorporated. One at a time, add in your milk, water and oil, mixing after each addition, and mix until smooth. Fold in your chopped peanuts.

Fill your cupcake liners two-thirds full with batter. Bake for 18 to 20 minutes until a toothpick inserted in the center comes out clean and the tops of the cupcakes spring back when touched. Remove from the oven to cool.

To make the frosting, whisk together the chocolate pudding and powdered sugar. Pour in the milk and whisk until thickened, about 3 to 5 minutes. Fold in your whipped topping, and refrigerate until ready to use.

Once the cupcakes are cool, add your frosting to a large piping bag fitted with an open star tip. Pipe swirls around the tops of each cupcake. Top with chopped peanuts and mini marshmallows, and drizzle over some chocolate syrup. Refrigerate any leftovers.

BANANAS FOSTER CUPCAKES

If I could eat bananas every day for the rest of my life I would. Combine bananas
and caramel together, and it takes you to a whole different level. These Bananas Foster Cupcakes
are a light and delicious banana cupcake with dulce de leche and rum frosting,
making these cupcakes simply irresistible.

MAKES 12 TO 14

1½ cups (180 g) all-purpose flour

1 tsp baking powder

1 tsp baking soda

½ tsp salt

¼ cup (60 ml) vegetable oil

½ cup (100 g) granulated sugar

¼ cup (45 g) brown sugar

1½ cups (450 g) bananas, mashed

1 egg

1 tsp vanilla extract

FROSTING

1 cup (240 g) unsalted butter,
softened

½ cup (120 g) dulce de leche or
caramel sauce

4 cups (400 g) powdered sugar

2-3 tbsp (30-45 ml) milk

½-1 tsp rum extract

Sliced bananas, for garnish
(optional, but highly
recommended!)

Preheat the oven to 350°F (177°C, or gas mark 4). Line a 12-count
cupcake pan with liners. Set aside.

In a medium bowl, whisk together your flour, baking powder, baking
soda and salt. Set aside.

In a stand mixer, mix together your vegetable oil and both sugars until
combined. Add in your bananas, egg and vanilla. Mix until blended,
then slowly add in your flour mixture.

Fill your cupcake liners two-thirds full with batter. Bake for 18 to
20 minutes until a toothpick inserted in the center comes out clean
and the tops of the cupcakes spring back when touched. Remove
from the oven to cool.

To make the frosting, in a stand mixer, add your butter and beat
until smooth. Add in your dulce de leche, and continue beating until
combined. Add in your powdered sugar 1 cup (100 g) at a time until
blended. Add in the milk 1 tablespoon (15 ml) at a time until the desired
consistency is reached. Mix in your rum extract, adding in ½ teaspoon
first and taste to see if you'd like more. Place the frosting into a piping
bag fitted with an open star tip. Pipe swirls over the top of cooled
cupcakes. Garnish with sliced bananas, if desired.

VANILLA MILKSHAKE CUPCAKES

There's nothing like ice cream and cake . . . unless you can mix the two together. These Vanilla Milkshake Cupcakes combine the perfect duo into one deliciously sweet and tasty dessert.

—————————————— MAKES 12 ——————————————

1½ cups (180 g) all-purpose flour

1½ tsp (6 g) baking powder

½ tsp salt

2 tbsp (30 g) malted milk powder

1 cup (240 g) unsalted butter, softened

⅔ cup (130 g) granulated sugar

2 eggs

2½ tsp (13 ml) vanilla extract

½ cup (120 ml) milk

FROSTING

1 cup (240 g) unsalted butter, softened

3 cups (300 g) powdered sugar

¼ cup (60 g) malted milk powder

1–2 tbsp (15–30 ml) milk, if needed

Malted milk balls for topping (optional)

Preheat the oven to 350°F (177°C, or gas mark 4). Line a 12-count muffin tin with cupcake liners. Set aside.

In a small bowl, whisk together your flour, baking powder, salt and milk powder. Set aside.

In a stand mixer, beat together your butter and sugar until fluffy. Add in the eggs one at a time, making sure each is incorporated after each addition. Mix in your vanilla. Alternate adding your dry ingredients and milk until fully combined.

Fill your cupcake liners two-thirds full. Bake for 18 to 20 minutes until a toothpick comes out clean and the tops of the cupcakes spring back when touched. Remove from the oven and let cool.

To make the frosting, in a stand mixer, beat your butter until smooth. Add in your powdered sugar 1 cup (100 g) at a time until combined. Add in your milk powder until blended. Lastly, add in the milk if needed to reach your desired consistency. Add your frosting to a piping bag fitted with a round tip. Pipe swirls on top of the cooled cupcakes. Top with malted milk balls, if desired.

COCONUT CREAM PIE CUPCAKES

I'm a coconut lover at heart. Coconut cream pie was one pie that my mom made growing up, and I soon became addicted. These Coconut Cream Pie Cupcakes are a triple threat with coconut cake, coconut frosting and a toasted coconut topping.

MAKES 12 TO 14

1¼ cups (150 g) all-purpose flour

1 cup (200 g) granulated sugar

1½ tsp (6 g) baking powder

½ tsp salt

½ cup (120 ml) coconut milk

2½ tsp (13 ml) vanilla extract

¼ cup (60 ml) vegetable oil

1 egg

½ cup (120 ml) water

FROSTING

2 cups (475 ml) heavy whipping cream

1 (3.4-oz [96-g]) package coconut cream pudding

¼ cup (25 g) powdered sugar

Toasted coconut, for garnish

Preheat the oven to 350°F (177°C, or gas mark 4). Line a 12-count cupcake pan with liners. Set aside.

In a stand mixer, mix together your flour, sugar, baking powder and salt until combined. Add in your coconut milk, vanilla, oil, egg and water, and mix until blended.

Fill the cupcake liners two-thirds full with batter. Bake in the oven for 18 to 20 minutes until a toothpick inserted in the center comes out clean and the tops of the cupcakes spring back when touched. Remove from the oven, and set aside to cool.

To make the frosting, add your heavy cream to a stand mixer. Beat on high until stiff peaks form. Fold in your coconut cream pudding and powdered sugar until blended. Add the frosting to a piping bag fitted with an open star tip. Pipe swirls over the tops of the cooled cupcakes. Top with toasted coconut.

MOCHA FRAPPE CUPCAKES

I'm a huge fan of coffee-flavored desserts. These Mocha Frappe Cupcakes take two of the best flavors—chocolate and coffee—and mash them up into one tasty cupcake. A moist and irresistible chocolate cupcake is frosted with a coffee buttercream and topped with chocolate-covered espresso beans.

─────────────── MAKES 14 ───────────────

1 cup (120 g) all-purpose flour

½ cup (50 g) unsweetened cocoa powder

1 tsp baking powder

½ tsp baking soda

½ tsp salt

1 cup (200 g) granulated sugar

2 eggs

½ cup (120 ml) milk

¼ cup (60 ml) vegetable oil

1 tsp vanilla extract

½ cup (120 ml) coffee

FROSTING

1 cup (240 g) unsalted butter, softened

3 tbsp (10 g) instant coffee granules

3 tsp (15 ml) water

3–4 cups (300–400 ml) powdered sugar

2–4 tbsp (30–60 ml) milk

Chocolate-covered espresso beans, for garnish (optional)

Preheat the oven to 350°F (177°C, or gas mark 4). Line a standard cupcake pan with cupcake liners. Set aside.

In a stand mixer, whisk together your flour, cocoa powder, baking powder, baking soda, salt and sugar. Add in your eggs one at a time until incorporated. Add in your milk, vegetable oil, vanilla and coffee, and mix until smooth.

Fill your cupcake liners two-thirds full with batter. Bake for 18 minutes until a toothpick inserted in the center comes out clean and the tops of the cupcakes spring back when touched. Remove from the oven to cool.

To make the frosting, in a stand mixer, beat your butter until smooth. In a small bowl, dissolve your coffee granules in the water. Add the coffee into your butter and beat until combined. Add in the powdered sugar 1 cup (100 g) at a time until blended. Add the milk 1 tablespoon (15 ml) at a time until the desired consistency is reached. Add your frosting to a piping bag fitted with an open star tip. Pipe swirls over the top of each cupcake, and top with chocolate-covered espresso beans, if desired.

WATERGATE CUPCAKES

If you've never had Grandma bring Watergate salad to a family function, you're truly missing out on this weird-but-delicious dessert. Pistachio, pineapple and coconut collide to make this delicious cake. It's frosted with a marshmallow buttercream frosting and topped with some coconut and pecans to finish it off.

—————————————————————— MAKES 12 ——————————————————————

1½ cups (180 g) all-purpose flour

1 tsp baking powder

½ tsp baking soda

½ tsp salt

⅔ cup (130 g) granulated sugar

½ cup (120 ml) oil

2 tsp (10 ml) vanilla extract

2 eggs

½ cup (120 ml) milk

1 (3.4-oz [96-g]) package pistachio pudding

1 (8-oz [227-g]) can crushed pineapple

½ cup (38 g) shredded coconut

FROSTING

1 cup (240 g) unsalted butter, softened

1 (7-oz [198-g]) container marshmallow fluff

1 tsp vanilla extract

2 cups (200 g) powdered sugar

Shredded coconut, for garnish (optional)

Chopped pecans, for garnish (optional)

Preheat the oven to 350°F (177°C, or gas mark 4). Line a 12-count cupcake pan with liners. Set aside.

In a stand mixer, add your flour, baking powder, baking soda, salt and sugar. Mix until blended. Add in your oil, vanilla, eggs and milk and mix until incorporated. Mix in the pistachio pudding, pineapple and coconut, and mix until blended.

Fill your liners two-thirds full with batter. Bake for 18 to 20 minutes until a toothpick inserted in the center comes out clean and the tops of the cupcakes spring back when touched. Remove from the oven to cool.

To make the frosting, in a stand mixer, beat your butter until smooth. Add in your marshmallow fluff and vanilla, and beat until incorporated. Add in your powdered sugar 1 cup (100 g) at a time. Place the frosting in a large piping bag fitted with a French star tip. Pipe swirls onto the tops of the cooled cupcakes.

Top with shredded coconut and chopped pecans, if desired.

SNOWBALL CUPCAKES

One of my son's favorite snacks has always been chocolate snowballs! In all honesty, I find them quite addictive myself. So why not make the kids' snack into a cupcake? A moist chocolate cupcake is topped with homemade marshmallow fluff and dipped in shredded coconut.

MAKES 12 TO 14

1 cup (120 g) all-purpose flour

1 cup (200 g) granulated sugar

½ cup (50 g) unsweetened cocoa powder

1 tsp baking powder

½ tsp baking soda

½ tsp salt

1 tsp vanilla extract

2 eggs

½ cup (120 ml) milk

½ cup (120 ml) water

¼ cup (60 ml) oil

FROSTING

¼ cup (60 ml) water

¾ cup (150 g) granulated sugar

¾ cup (180 ml) corn syrup

2 egg whites

¼ tsp cream of tartar

2 tsp (10 ml) vanilla extract

1½ cups (115 g) shredded coconut

Preheat the oven to 350°F (177°C, or gas mark 4). Line a standard cupcake pan with cupcake liners. Set aside.

In a stand mixer, add your flour, sugar, cocoa powder, baking powder, baking soda and salt. Mix together until blended. Add in your vanilla and eggs until incorporated. One at a time, add in your milk, water and oil, mixing well after each addition until smooth.

Fill your cupcake liners two-thirds full with batter. Bake for 18 to 20 minutes until a toothpick inserted in the center comes out clean and the tops of the cupcakes spring back when touched. Remove from the oven to cool.

To make the frosting, in a saucepan, heat the water, sugar and corn syrup over medium-high heat, whisking occasionally until a candy thermometer inserted into the mixture reaches 240°F (116°C). While the sugar mixture boils, beat together your egg whites and cream of tartar in a stand mixer fitted with paddle attachment until soft peaks form. Once the sugar mixture reaches 240°F (116°C), place your mixer on low and slowly stream in the mixture. When all combined, turn your mixer to high and beat until stiff peaks form, about 5 to 7 minutes. The frosting should be thick and glossy. Add in your vanilla, and beat for 1 more minute.

Place your shredded coconut in a large bowl. Spread a large dollop of frosting on top of the cupcakes, and dip them into the coconut to coat.

PEANUT BUTTER BLOSSOM CUPCAKES

Who doesn't love the classic peanut butter blossom cookie? How about taking that cookie and turning it into a cupcake? A peanut butter cake is filled with a creamy chocolate ganache and frosted with a smooth-and-tasty peanut butter buttercream. It's topped off with more of the filling, making this cupcake a peanut butter and chocolate explosion.

MAKES 12 TO 14

½ cup (120 g) unsalted butter, softened

½ cup (90 g) creamy peanut butter

¼ cup (50 g) granulated sugar

¼ cup (45 g) brown sugar

2 eggs

1½ tsp (8 ml) vanilla extract

1½ cups (180 g) all-purpose flour

1 tsp baking powder

½ tsp salt

⅔ cup (160 ml) milk

FILLING

1 cup (175 g) semi-sweet chocolate chips

¼ cup (60 ml) heavy cream

FROSTING

1 cup (240 g) unsalted butter, softened

1 cup (180 g) creamy peanut butter

4 cups (400 g) powdered sugar

¼ cup (60 ml) milk

Preheat the oven to 350°F (177°C, or gas mark 4). Line a cupcake pan with liners. Set aside.

In a stand mixer, beat together your butter and peanut butter until smooth. Add in your granulated sugar, brown sugar, eggs and vanilla. Continue to beat until blended.

In another bowl, whisk together your flour, baking powder and salt. Alternate adding dry ingredients and milk until it comes together.

Fill the cupcake liners two-thirds full with batter. Bake for 18 to 22 minutes until a toothpick inserted in a center comes out clean and the tops of the cupcakes spring back when touched. Remove from the oven to cool.

To make the filling, place your chocolate chips in a heat-safe bowl. Set aside.

In a microwave-safe bowl, add your heavy cream. Heat in the microwave for about 1 minute until bubbling. Pour over the chocolate chips, and let sit for 5 minutes. Whisk your chocolate and cream mixture until it becomes smooth. Set aside to cool and thicken slightly.

Using a cupcake corer or melon baller, remove the centers of the cupcakes. Spoon your filling evenly into each cupcake, reserving a few tablespoons for drizzling. Once filled, set aside to cool more.

To make your frosting, in a stand mixer, beat your butter and peanut butter together until smooth. Add in your powdered sugar 1 cup (100 g) at a time. Add in your milk and beat until creamy. Add your frosting to a piping bag fitted with an open star tip. Pipe swirls over the tops of the cupcakes.

Place your remaining filling mixture in a small zip-top bag and cut the corner off. Drizzle over the tops of the cupcakes.

CHOCOLATE-COVERED STRAWBERRY CUPCAKES

Who says chocolate-covered strawberries are only for special occasions? When it comes to these easy peasy cupcakes, you'll want to make them all the time. A rich and delicious chocolate cupcake is frosted with an oh-so-heavenly strawberry buttercream and drizzled with some chocolate syrup.

──────────────── MAKES 14 TO 16 ────────────────

1 cup (120 g) all-purpose flour

1 cup (200 g) granulated sugar

½ cup (50 g) unsweetened cocoa powder

1 tsp baking powder

½ tsp baking soda

½ tsp salt

1 tsp vanilla extract

2 eggs

½ cup (120 ml) milk

½ cup (120 ml) water

¼ cup (60 ml) vegetable oil

FROSTING

1 cup (240 g) unsalted butter, softened

4 cups (400 g) powdered sugar

½ cup (100 g) diced strawberries

Chocolate syrup, for garnish

Preheat the oven to 350°F (177°C, or gas mark 4). Line a 12-count cupcake pan with liners. Set aside.

In a stand mixer, add your flour, sugar, cocoa powder, baking powder, baking soda and salt. Mix together until blended. Add in your vanilla and eggs, and mix until combined. One at a time, add in your milk, water and oil, mixing well after each addition.

Fill your cupcake liners two-thirds full with batter. Bake for 18 to 20 minutes until a toothpick inserted in the center comes out clean and the tops of the cupcakes spring back when touched. Remove from the oven to cool.

To make the frosting, in a stand mixer, beat your butter until smooth. Add in your powdered sugar 1 cup (100 g) at a time until combined. Add your strawberries to a small food processor and process until pureed. Pour the puree into your frosting mixture, and beat until blended. Place the frosting in a large piping bag fitted with an open star tip. Pipe swirls over the cooled cupcakes.

Drizzle with chocolate syrup.

HUMMINGBIRD CUPCAKES

There are so many components and flavors to this cupcake that it is hard to resist. Banana, pineapple, coconut and pecans make the base of this tasty cake. Top it all off with a light cream cheese frosting and you are sent to flavor town!

MAKES 12 TO 14

1½ cups (180 g) all-purpose flour

½ tsp baking soda

½ tsp salt

½ tsp cinnamon

¾ cup (150 g) granulated sugar

¼ cup (45 g) brown sugar

2 eggs

½ cup (120 ml) vegetable oil

1½ tsp (8 ml) vanilla extract

1 cup (230 g) bananas, mashed

½ cup (115 g) crushed pineapple

½ cup (50 g) shredded coconut

½ cup (75 g) chopped pecans

FROSTING

½ cup (120 g) unsalted butter, softened

1 (8-oz [230-g]) package cream cheese, softened

4 cups (400 g) powdered sugar

1 tsp vanilla extract

Pecans, for garnish (optional)

Preheat the oven to 350°F (177°C, or gas mark 4). Line a 12-count cupcake pan with liners. Set aside.

In a bowl, whisk together the flour, baking soda, salt and cinnamon. Set aside.

In a stand mixer, add your granulated sugar, brown sugar, eggs, oil and vanilla. Beat until blended. Slowly add in your dry ingredients, and mix until combined. Add in your bananas, pineapple, coconut and pecans, and beat until incorporated.

Fill the cupcake liners two-thirds full with batter. Bake for 18 to 20 minutes until a toothpick inserted in the center comes out clean and the tops of the cupcakes spring back when touched. Remove from the oven to cool.

To make the frosting, in a stand mixer, beat together your butter and cream cheese until blended and smooth. Add in your powdered sugar 1 cup (100 g) at a time, then mix in your vanilla. Place the frosting in a large piping bag fitted with a French star tip. Pipe swirls over the top of the cupcakes and top with pecans, if desired.

SWEET

BEGINNINGS

If you live for breakfast and love sweets, then this chapter is
for you! Full of delicious donuts, waffles, pastries and more,
this section offers a variety of options for your sweet tooth.
You will find a fun Glazed Donut Breakfast Bake (page 179)
and a Crème Brûlée French Toast Bake (page 160), along
with an addicting Cinnamon Roll Bread Pudding (page 175).
They say breakfast is an essential part of the day,
and I think that starting my day off in a sweet
way is the best way to wake up.

CRÈME BRÛLÉE FRENCH TOAST BAKE

When you combine French toast and caramelized sugar, there is no greater flavor out there. Add a twist of orange to really set it off, and you have the makings of an irresistible breakfast that is great for the whole family.

MAKES 6 TO 8

1½ cups (350 ml) heavy cream

5 eggs

1 tsp vanilla extract

1 tsp orange extract

¼ tsp salt

½ cup (120 g) unsalted butter

1 cup (180 g) brown sugar

2 tbsp (30 ml) corn syrup

1 (16-oz [450-g]) loaf French bread, ends discarded and cut into 12 (1-inch [2.5-cm]) slices

Powdered sugar, for garnish (optional)

In a large bowl, whisk together your heavy cream, eggs, vanilla, orange extract and salt. Set aside.

In a medium pot on the stove, melt together your butter, brown sugar and corn syrup until smooth, about 2 to 3 minutes. Pour the brown sugar mixture into the bottom of a 9 x 13–inch (23 x 33–cm) baking dish.

Dunk each of your bread slices into your egg mixture, then shingle them in rows of 6 into your baking dish on top of your brown sugar mixture. Pour the remaining egg mixture over the top and cover. Refrigerate for 8 hours to overnight.

Remove from the refrigerator, and let come to room temperature.

Preheat the oven to 350°F (177°C, or gas mark 4).

Bake your French toast bake for 40 minutes. Remove from the oven, and let it cool for 5 minutes. Cut out slices and flip over onto a plate, with the brown sugar side up. Drizzle with some of the leftover brown sugar, and dust with powdered sugar, if desired.

COCONUT CARAMEL COOKIE WAFFLES

Caramel, chocolate and coconut are just the beginning of these delicious and easy waffles!
A rich-and-light chocolate waffle is topped with toasted coconut and caramel sauce,
turning a traditional breakfast into a serious flavor experience.

MAKES 6 TO 8

2 cups (240 g) all-purpose flour

⅓ cup (37 g) cocoa powder

⅓ cup (65 g) granulated sugar

½ tsp salt

2 tsp (7 g) baking powder

1 tsp baking soda

2 eggs

⅓ cup (80 g) unsalted butter, melted

2 cups (475 ml) buttermilk

1 tsp vanilla extract

1 cup (75 g) shredded coconut

Toasted coconut, for garnish

Caramel sauce, for garnish

Preheat a waffle maker to the high setting.

In a large bowl, whisk together your flour, cocoa powder, sugar, salt, baking powder and baking soda. In another bowl, whisk together your eggs, butter, buttermilk and vanilla. Add your wet ingredients into your dry, and whisk together. Fold in your shredded coconut.

Spray your waffle maker with nonstick cooking spray. Ladle ½ cup (120 ml) of batter into your preheated waffle maker, and cook for about 3 minutes. Remove the cooked waffle, and transfer to a baking sheet. Repeat with the remaining batter.

Sprinkle with toasted coconut, and drizzle with caramel sauce.

CARROT CAKE SCONES

We love carrot cake around this house. Any way that I can incorporate one of our favorite cake flavors into our morning routine is a necessity. These scones are light, moist and packed full of flavor, and they're topped off with a sweet and creamy cream cheese glaze.

———————————————— MAKES 8 ————————————————

2 cups (240 g) all-purpose flour

¼ cup (50 g) granulated sugar

¼ cup (45 g) brown sugar

1 tbsp (11 g) baking powder

¼ tsp salt

1 tsp cinnamon

1 tsp nutmeg

¼ tsp ground cloves

½ cup (120 g) unsalted butter, softened and cut into cubes

½ cup (60 g) sour cream

½ cup (120 ml) milk

1 egg

1 tsp vanilla extract

½ cup (55 g) shredded carrots

½ cup (37 g) shredded coconut

GLAZE

1 oz (28 g) cream cheese, softened

1 cup (100 g) powdered sugar

2 tbsp (30 ml) milk

½ cup (60 g) chopped pecans, for garnish

Preheat the oven to 350°F (177°C, or gas mark 4). Line a baking sheet with parchment paper. Set aside.

In a large bowl, whisk together your flour, sugars, baking powder, salt, cinnamon, nutmeg and ground cloves. Cut in your butter with a pastry blender until small crumbs form.

In another bowl, stir together your sour cream, milk, egg and vanilla. Stir the wet mixture into the dry ingredients until just moistened. Fold in your carrots and coconut.

Turn out onto a lightly-floured surface and knead a few times until it comes together. Press into an 8- to 9-inch (20- to 23-cm) circle and cut into 8 equal-size wedges. Place the wedges on the prepared baking sheet. Bake in the oven for 15 to 18 minutes, until slightly golden.

Remove the scones from the oven to cool.

To make the glaze, whisk together the cream cheese, powdered sugar and milk in a small bowl. Drizzle it over the top of the cooled scones, and sprinkle with chopped pecans.

OVERNIGHT CHERRY CHEESECAKE OATS

Cherries and cheesecake always go hand in hand. Sometimes you want an early morning treat that takes little effort to whip together, and this recipe is just that. Toss everything in a bowl and let it sit overnight. In the morning, you wake up to something you can hardly resist.

MAKES 4 TO 6

2 cups (200 g) old-fashioned oats

2 cups (475 ml) milk

½ cup (143 g) vanilla Greek yogurt

¼–½ cup (45–90 g) brown sugar

1 tsp vanilla extract

1 (21-oz [595-g]) can cherry pie filling

Graham cracker crumbs, for garnish

In a large bowl, add your oats. In another bowl, whisk together your milk, Greek yogurt, brown sugar and vanilla. Pour the yogurt mixture over your oats. Stir in your cherry pie filling and cover. Place in the refrigerator for at least 8 hours.

Remove the oats from the refrigerator, and top with the graham cracker crumbs.

To serve in cups, place about ¼ cup (22 g) graham crackers in the bottom of each of the cups. Layer with oats and sprinkle with additional graham cracker crumbs.

To serve in bowls, just sprinkle with crumbs.

FUNFETTI WAFFLES

Having four kids and switching up our breakfast routine can be challenging sometimes. But when you take one of your favorite cakes and turn it into a waffle, you won't have any leftovers. These simple Funfetti Waffles whip up fast, and they are gone within minutes.

MAKES 6 TO 8

2 cups (240 g) all-purpose flour

½ tsp salt

4 tsp (15 g) baking powder

3 tbsp (38 g) granulated sugar

2 eggs

2 cups (475 ml) buttermilk

⅓ cup (80 g) unsalted butter, melted

2 tsp (10 ml) vanilla extract

½ cup (80 g) rainbow sprinkles, plus more for garnish (optional)

ICING

4 oz (113 g) cream cheese, softened

4 tbsp (60 g) unsalted butter, softened

1½ cups (150 g) powdered sugar

6 tbsp (90 ml) milk

½ tsp vanilla extract

Whipped cream, optional

In a large bowl, whisk together your flour, salt, baking powder and sugar. In a medium bowl, whisk together your eggs, buttermilk, butter and vanilla. Stir your wet ingredients into your dry ingredients, then fold in your rainbow sprinkles.

Spray a waffle iron with nonstick cooking spray. Ladle about ½ cup (120 ml) of batter onto the center, and spread it out thin. Close the waffle iron, and cook for about 3 minutes or until golden. Repeat with the remaining batter.

To make the icing, whisk together the cream cheese and butter until smooth. Add in the powdered sugar, milk and vanilla extract and whisk until combined.

Drizzle on top of the waffles. Top with whipped cream and additional sprinkles, if desired.

BAKED APPLE PIE DONUTS

What's more classic than an apple pie? How about having apple pie for breakfast? These Baked Apple Pie Donuts have chunks of apple baked right in, and the cinnamon-sugar topping makes it hard to keep from having just one!

MAKES 6 TO 8

1 cup (120 g) all-purpose flour

1 tsp baking powder

¼ cup (50 g) granulated sugar

1 egg

¼ cup (30 g) sour cream

¼ cup (60 ml) milk

1 tbsp (15 g) unsalted butter, melted

1 tsp vanilla extract

1 cup (120 g) finely diced apples

TOPPING

¼ cup (60 g) unsalted butter, melted

2 tbsp (25 g) granulated sugar

½ tsp cinnamon

Preheat the oven to 400°F (204°C). Spray a standard donut pan with nonstick cooking spray. Set aside.

In a medium bowl, whisk together your flour, baking powder and sugar. Add in your egg, sour cream, milk, butter and vanilla. Whisk until blended. Fold in your diced apples.

Add your donut batter to a piping bag and cut off the tip. Pipe into the wells of the donut pan.

Bake in the oven for 10 minutes until slightly golden. Remove the donuts from the oven, and let them cool slightly before removing to a cooling rack.

To make the topping, melt your butter in a small bowl. In another small bowl, whisk together your sugar and cinnamon. Dip the tops of the donuts in the butter, then into the cinnamon mixture.

STRAWBERRY CHEESECAKE BAKED OATMEAL

Strawberries are never hard to find in my house. When it comes to breakfast, they are a staple. Since cheesecake is one of our favorite desserts, breakfast that includes a creamy swirled cheesecake is a winner in my book. This Strawberry Cheesecake Baked Oatmeal is full of all the dessert flavors with a spin just for your morning routine.

MAKES 6 TO 8

3 cups (300 g) old-fashioned oats

1½ tsp (6 g) baking powder

½ tsp salt

½ cup (100 g) granulated sugar

½ cup (90 g) brown sugar

1½ tsp (4 g) cinnamon

2 eggs

2½ cups (300 ml) milk

1 tsp vanilla extract

2 cups (400 g) sliced strawberries

CHEESECAKE FILLING

1 (8-oz [230-g]) block cream cheese, softened

⅓ cup (40 g) sour cream

½ cup (100 g) granulated sugar

½ tsp vanilla extract

1 egg

Preheat the oven to 350°F (177°C, or gas mark 4).

In a large bowl, combine together your oats, baking powder, salt, granulated sugar, brown sugar and cinnamon. In another bowl, whisk together your eggs, milk and vanilla. Set aside.

To make the cheesecake filling, beat together your cream cheese and sour cream until smooth. Add in your sugar, vanilla and egg until combined. Set aside.

Spray a 9 x 13–inch (23 x 33–cm) pan with nonstick cooking spray. Spread half of your oat mixture over the bottom. Top with half of your sliced strawberries, then dollop half of your cheesecake mixture over the strawberries. Spread the remaining oats over the top, and pour your milk-and-egg mixture over that. Top with the remaining strawberries, and dollop with the remaining cheesecake filling.

Swirl the cheesecake gently through the top layer of your oats, making sure that it is evenly distributed so you have cheesecake throughout the whole dish.

Bake for 40 minutes until set.

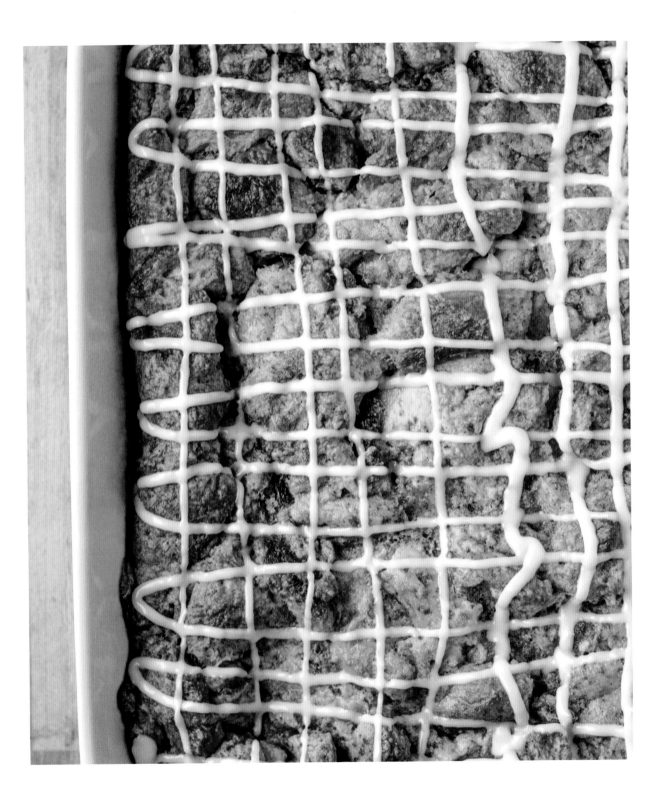

CINNAMON ROLL BREAD PUDDING

Cinnamon rolls are a staple breakfast food in my house. My kids gobble them up quicker than they appear! This bread pudding version gives an adult spin on a classic breakfast treat, turning your favorite into a delicious, gooey delight!

MAKES 6 TO 8

2 (8-count) packages refrigerated cinnamon rolls, baked and cooled

1 cup (240 ml) milk

1½ cups (350 ml) heavy cream

5 eggs

¼ cup (50 g) sugar

1 tsp (5 ml) vanilla extract

½ tsp cinnamon

GLAZE

1 cup (100 g) powdered sugar

2-3 tbsp (30-45 ml) milk

Chop up your cinnamon rolls into 1-inch (2.5-cm) pieces, and add them to a large bowl. In another bowl, whisk together your milk, cream, eggs, sugar, vanilla and cinnamon until combined. Pour the mixture over your cinnamon roll pieces, and stir to combine and coat. Let sit for 15 to 20 minutes to soak up the liquid.

Preheat the oven to 350°F (177°C, or gas mark 4).

Spray a 9 x 13-inch (23 x 33-cm) baking dish with nonstick cooking spray. Pour your cinnamon roll mixture into the prepared baking dish. Bake in the oven for 1 hour until the center is set.

Remove the bread pudding from the oven and let cool slightly. In a small bowl, whisk together your powdered sugar and milk. Drizzle over the bread pudding.

BANANA BREAD OATMEAL

If I had to choose one bread that I could eat over and over again, it would hands down be banana bread. This Banana Bread Oatmeal is packed full of all of the flavors of your typical bread, and it's made into a breakfast treat that will quickly become a morning favorite.

───────────────── MAKES 2 TO 3 ─────────────────

2 medium bananas, mashed

½ cup (90 g) brown sugar, extra for topping if desired

½ tsp vanilla extract

½ tsp cinnamon

1¼ cups (300 ml) water

1¼ cups (300 ml) milk

2½ cups (250 g) old-fashioned oats

Sliced bananas, for garnish (optional)

Chopped pecans or walnuts, for garnish (optional)

In a medium bowl, stir together your bananas, brown sugar, vanilla and cinnamon. Set aside.

In a medium-sized pot on the stove, add your water and milk, and bring to a boil. Stir in your oats and heat for about 3 minutes, continuously stirring until the liquid is absorbed. Stir in your banana mixture, and continue to heat until the oats are tender, about 2 to 3 minutes.

Remove from the heat, and let cool slightly. Top with the banana, brown sugar and chopped pecans, if desired.

SNICKERDOODLE PANCAKES

If you want an easy and flavorful breakfast, these pancakes are it! Light and fluffy and coated in cinnamon sugar, they have all the flavors of the traditional cookie but in pancake form.

— MAKES 6 —

1½ cups (180 g) all-purpose flour

2 tbsp (25 g) granulated sugar

1 tbsp (11 g) baking powder

1 tsp salt

1 tsp cinnamon

1¼ cups (300 ml) milk, warmed

1 egg

¼ cup (60 g) unsalted butter, melted

1 tsp vanilla extract

TOPPING

½ tsp cinnamon

2 tbsp (25 g) granulated sugar

¼ cup (60 g) unsalted butter, melted

In a large bowl, whisk together your flour, sugar, baking powder, salt and cinnamon. Stir in your milk, egg, butter and vanilla, and whisk until almost smooth. Do not overmix.

In a large skillet or griddle pan over medium heat, add a little butter and swirl it around so it coats the surface. Using a ⅓-cup (80-ml) measuring cup, scoop out pancake mixture, pour it onto the skillet, and spread out gently. Cook until little bubbles start to form on top of the pancake surface, about 2 to 3 minutes. Flip and cook for another 1 to 2 minutes. Remove the pancakes from the pan, and place them on a plate. Repeat with the remaining batter.

To make your topping, mix together your cinnamon and sugar. When ready to serve, brush the tops of the pancakes with butter and sprinkle with the cinnamon-sugar mixture.

GLAZED DONUT BREAKFAST BAKE

Who thought glazed donuts couldn't get better? Toss them with some milk, cream and eggs, and then bake them up, and you have yourself a recipe that you will want to keep for years. Add a light and flavorful vanilla glaze to the top and you won't want to stop with this breakfast bake.

MAKES 6 TO 8

2 (10.5-oz [298-g]) packages mini glazed donuts

4 eggs

1 cup (240 ml) milk

1 cup (240 ml) heavy cream

½ cup (100 g) granulated sugar

1 tsp vanilla extract

½ tsp cinnamon

TOPPING

1 cup (100 g) powdered sugar

1 tsp vanilla extract

2–3 tsp (10–15 ml) water

Preheat the oven to 350°F (177°C, or gas mark 4). Grease a 9 x 13–inch (23 x 33–cm) baking dish with nonstick cooking spray. Set aside.

Cut your donuts into quarters, and place them in a large bowl. In another bowl, whisk together your eggs, milk, cream, sugar, vanilla and cinnamon. Pour the mixture over the donuts, and stir to coat. Let the mixture sit for 20 minutes to soak up the liquid.

Spread the mixture into the prepared baking dish, and bake for 1 hour. Remove the donut bake from the oven, and let it cool slightly.

To make topping, in a small bowl, whisk together your powdered sugar, vanilla and water. Drizzle over the donut bake.

ELVIS CINNAMON ROLLS

These cinnamon rolls are something else, let me tell you! Spread with brown sugar, cinnamon and butter and filled with diced banana and bacon, there is nothing normal about these. Top them off with a peanut butter glaze, and you have yourself a breakfast worthy of the king!

──────── MAKES 12 ────────

DOUGH

½ cup (120 g) unsalted butter

1 cup (240 ml) milk

¼ cup (50 g) granulated sugar

1 (0.25-oz [21-g]) package active dry yeast

½ tsp salt

3½ cups (420 g) all-purpose flour

1 egg

FILLING

1 cup (180 g) brown sugar

2 tsp (5 g) cinnamon

¼ cup (60 g) unsalted butter, softened

1 large banana, diced

6 slices bacon, cooked and crumbled

GLAZE

½ cup (90 g) peanut butter, melted

1 cup (100 g) powdered sugar

¼ cup (60 ml) milk

Melt together the butter and milk on the stovetop on medium-high heat, about 2 to 3 minutes. Remove from the heat. Add in your sugar, and let cool to 105 to 110°F (41 to 43°C). Once cooled, add in your yeast and dissolve. Let proof for 10 minutes.

Pour the yeast mixture into the bowl of a stand mixer fitted with a dough hook.

Add in the salt, flour and egg. Mix on medium until the dough pulls away from the side.

Spray a large bowl with nonstick cooking spray, and place the dough into the bowl. Cover and let rise until doubled in size, about 1 hour. Grease a 9 x 13–inch (23 x 33–cm) baking dish. Set aside.

Once the dough has risen, lightly flour a work surface. Turn the dough out onto the surface, and roll into a 13 x 17–inch (33 x 43–cm) rectangle.

In a small bowl, whisk together your brown sugar and cinnamon. Set aside. Spread your butter over your dough, and sprinkle with the brown sugar mixture. Top with your diced bananas and crumbled bacon, and roll up tightly starting on the long side. Trim the edges off, then cut into 12 equal pieces.

Place the 12 pieces in the prepared baking dish. Cover and let rise until doubled in size, about 1 hour.

Preheat the oven to 350°F (177°C, or gas mark 4) and bake for 25 minutes until golden brown. Remove the rolls from the oven, and let them cool slightly, about 10 minutes.

To make your glaze, mix together your peanut butter, powdered sugar and milk. Drizzle over the warm rolls.

BAKED CINNAMON ROLL DONUTS

We've never been a family to come across a donut that we don't instantly fall in love with. Mashing up two of our favorite breakfast staples was a must. These donuts are baked with a cinnamon roll filling right on top and then glazed, making them a winning breakfast.

———————————————— MAKES 6 TO 8 ————————————————

1 cup (120 g) all-purpose flour

1 tsp baking powder

¼ cup (50 g) granulated sugar

1 egg

¼ cup (30 g) sour cream

¼ cup (60 ml) milk

1 tbsp (15 g) unsalted butter, melted

1 tsp vanilla extract

TOPPING

2 tbsp (30 g) unsalted butter

1 tsp cinnamon

¼ cup (45 g) brown sugar

1 tsp cornstarch

1 tsp milk

1 tsp vanilla extract

ICING

½ cup (50 g) powdered sugar

2 tbsp (30 ml) milk

Preheat the oven to 400°F (204°C). Spray a standard donut pan with nonstick cooking spray. Set aside.

In a medium bowl, whisk together your flour, baking powder and sugar. Add in your egg, sour cream, milk, butter and vanilla. Whisk until blended.

For the topping, in a small saucepan over medium-low heat, melt together your butter, cinnamon, brown sugar, cornstarch and milk until smooth, about 2 to 3 minutes. Remove from the heat, and stir in your vanilla.

Spoon 1 to 2 tablespoons (15 to 30 ml) of topping into the wells of a donut pan. Place your donut batter into a piping bag and cut off the tip, then pipe the batter into the wells of the pan.

Bake in the oven for 10 minutes until slightly golden. Remove the donuts from the oven, and let them cool in the pan for 5 minutes before removing.

To make your icing, mix together your powdered sugar and milk in a bowl.

Remove the donuts from the pan and onto a cooling rack. Let cool for about 5 minutes more. Drizzle the icing over the tops of the donuts.

THIS
AND THAT

What do you do with fun desserts that you can't quite place?
Well, you give them their own delicious home of course. This
chapter is a mixture of fun dips, salads, dippers and anything
else that you can't quite find a particular place for. This little
spot of heaven holds an abundance of yumminess!

FRUITY PEBBLE CHURROS

If you don't already love Fruity Pebbles, you will now. Classic churros are whipped up
and tossed with crushed up Fruity Pebbles cereal and sugar, giving a fun nostalgic twist
to these favorite handheld treats.

MAKES 10 TO 12

1 cup (240 ml) water

½ tbsp (7 g) granulated sugar

5 tbsp (70 g) unsalted butter

½ tsp salt

1 cup (120 g) all-purpose flour

2 eggs

1 tsp vanilla extract

COATING

¼ cup (5 g) crushed fruity crisp
rice cereal, such as Fruity Pebbles

1 tbsp (13 g) granulated sugar

Preheat your deep fryer to 350°F (177°C).

In a saucepan, add your water, sugar, butter and salt. Heat on medium-high heat until the butter is melted and it comes to a slight boil. Turn the heat off. Add in the flour and stir vigorously until a ball forms and all the flour is incorporated. Place the flour ball in a stand mixer and let cool for 5 minutes.

In a small bowl, whisk together your eggs and vanilla. Once the ball has cooled, add half of your egg mixture and beat on medium speed until combined. Add the remaining egg mixture, and continue to beat until blended.

Add your dough to a large piping bag fitted with a French star tip. Mix together your crushed fruity cereal and sugar, and place it on a plate. Set aside.

In your deep fryer, pipe 6- to 8-inch (15- to 20-cm) strips directly into the hot oil. Fry for about 3 to 4 minutes until golden. Remove the churros from the deep fryer, place on a paper towel–lined plate to drain and repeat with the remaining dough. Sprinkle and roll in the coating mixture while still warm.

PUMPKIN SPICE LATTE DIP

When fall rolls around, I'm all about everything pumpkin-flavored, especially pumpkin spice lattes. Now how about turning a beloved drink into a sweet and filling dip? This Pumpkin Spice Latte Dip has hints of coffee and pumpkin, and it is just subtly sweet and perfect.

MAKES 4 TO 6

2 tsp (2 g) instant coffee granules

½ cup (120 ml) heavy cream

1 (8-oz [230-g]) package cream cheese, softened

1 cup (100 g) powdered sugar

2½ tsp (6 g) pumpkin pie spice

1 tsp vanilla extract

½ cup (120 ml) pumpkin puree

In a bowl, dissolve the coffee granules in the heavy cream by whisking them together.

In another bowl, beat the heavy cream mixture until stiff peaks form. Set aside.

In a stand mixer, beat together your cream cheese and powdered sugar until smooth. Add in the pumpkin pie spice and vanilla until blended. Gently mix in your pumpkin, then fold in your whipped cream mixture until combined. Chill before serving.

CHERRY PIE TAQUITOS

When we go out to our local Mexican joint I'm all about those beef taquitos.
But have you ever wanted to turn those delicious things into a sweet dish? Welcome these
Cherry Pie Taquitos. Stuffed with cherry pie filling and topped with a cinnamon-sugar mixture,
these are perfect for a Taco Tuesday dessert.

MAKES 6

2 tbsp (30 g) unsalted butter, melted and divided

6 medium flour tortillas

1 (21-oz [595-g]) can cherry pie filling

2 tbsp (25 g) granulated sugar

½ tsp cinnamon

Preheat the oven to 350°F (177°C, or gas mark 4). Brush the bottom of an 8 x 8-inch (20 x 20-cm) baking dish with 1 tablespoon (15 ml) of melted butter. Set aside.

Spread your tortillas evenly with pie filling, and roll them up. Place them seam-side down in the prepared pan. Brush with the remaining butter.

In a small bowl, mix together your sugar and cinnamon. Sprinkle over the top of the tortillas, then bake for 15 to 18 minutes until golden.

COOKIES-AND-CREAM PIZZA

Ever since I was a kid, I've been a fan of dessert pizzas. This cookies-and-cream version takes one of my favorite cookies and mashes it with my favorite dessert. The crust is studded with crushed cookies, and it's topped with a white chocolate–cream cheese frosting, sprinkled with more crushed cookies and white chocolate chips and finished with a drizzle of chocolate syrup.

SERVES 8 TO 10

½ cup (120 g) unsalted butter, softened

¾ cup (150 g) granulated sugar

1 egg

1 tsp vanilla extract

1½ cups (180 g) all-purpose flour

½ tsp salt

1 tsp baking powder

7 chocolate sandwich cookies, such as Oreos, crushed, plus more for garnish

TOPPING

1 (8-oz [230-g]) package cream cheese, softened

1 (4-oz [113-g]) white chocolate baking bar

3 cups (300 g) powdered sugar

White chocolate chips, for garnish

Chocolate syrup, for garnish

Preheat the oven to 350°F (177°C, or gas mark 4). Line a 10-inch (25-cm) pizza pan with parchment paper. Set aside.

In a stand mixer, beat together the butter and sugar until fluffy. Add in your egg and vanilla until combined.

In another bowl, whisk together your flour, salt and baking powder. Slowly add the dry ingredients to the butter mixture until combined. Lastly, add in your crushed cookies until blended.

Press into a large circle on the prepared baking sheet. Bake for 15 to 20 minutes until golden. Remove the pizza from the oven, and let it cool completely.

To make the topping, in a stand mixer, beat your cream cheese until smooth. Add your white chocolate to a microwave-safe bowl. Heat in the microwave in 30-second increments, stirring each time, until melted. Add the melted chocolate into the cream cheese, and beat until blended. Add the powdered sugar 1 cup (100 g) at a time until combined.

Spread the frosting over the cooled crust. Top with crushed cookies and white chocolate chips, and drizzle with the chocolate syrup.

FRENCH CRULLER DIPPERS

If I had to choose one donut to eat for the rest of my life, the French cruller would hands down be it. This twist on the classic treat makes them into dippers served with a tasty powdered sugar and honey sauce.

───────────────── MAKES 20 ─────────────────

6 tbsp (90 g) unsalted butter

1 cup (240 ml) water

2 tsp (10 g) granulated sugar

1 cup (120 g) all-purpose flour

3 eggs

2 egg whites

DIPPING SAUCE

1½ cups (150 g) powdered sugar

¼ cup (60 ml) milk

1 tbsp (15 ml) honey

Preheat a deep fryer to 365°F (185°C).

In a large pan over medium-high heat, whisk together your butter, water and sugar until boiling and the butter is melted, about 3 minutes. Once boiling vigorously, stir in your flour until it starts to take a ball shape. Continue to heat and stir for about 1 to 2 minutes to cook out the excess water. Remove from the pan, and place in a stand mixer fitted with the whisk attachment. Let cool 10 minutes. Turn the mixer on medium speed. Add in the eggs one at a time, mixing well after each addition.

In a small bowl, stir together your egg whites. Add them into the batter, and mix until combined. Once mixed, add the dough to a large piping bag fitted with an open star tip. Pipe 6-inch (15-cm) long strips into your deep fryer in batches of 3, cooking about 3 minutes on each side until golden brown. Remove from the deep fryer, and place on a paper towel–lined plate to drain. Repeat with the remaining batter.

To make the dipping sauce, mix together powdered sugar, milk and honey.

PECAN PIE GRANOLA

If you love the pie, then you'll love this little snacking treat! Full of all the classic flavors of the baked holiday treat, this granola is perfect for breakfast with yogurt or milk. Enjoy it as an on-the-go snack to keep your energy up or just something to have to munch on while sitting doing your Netflix binge.

SERVES 4 TO 6

2 cups (200 g) old-fashioned oats

1 cup (120 g) pecans, chopped

¼ cup (45 g) brown sugar

½ tsp salt

½ tsp cinnamon

½ tsp pumpkin pie spice

½ cup (120 ml) maple syrup

2 tbsp (30 ml) vegetable oil

Preheat the oven to 300°F (177°C). Line a baking sheet with parchment paper. Set aside.

In a large bowl, whisk together your dry ingredients. Set aside. In a small bowl, whisk together your wet ingredients. Pour the wet ingredients over the dry ingredients.

Spread the granola in an even layer onto the prepared baking sheet. Bake for 1 hour, stirring every 15 to 20 minutes. Remove the granola from the oven, and allow it to cool completely before serving.

LEMON BLUEBERRY CHEESECAKE SALAD

Cheesecake turned into a salad? Don't mind if I do! This summer treat has the creamy flavor of cheesecake filled with blueberries, pie pieces and a twist of lemon. It's the perfect way to wind down an afternoon picnic!

— SERVES 6 TO 8 —

2 (8-oz [230-g]) packages cream cheese, softened

1 cup (100 g) powdered sugar

2 cups (475 ml) heavy whipping cream

2 tsp (10 ml) lemon extract

1 (21-oz [595-g]) can blueberry pie filling

1–2 tsp (5–10 g) lemon zest (optional)

1 (9-inch [23-cm]) premade graham cracker pie crust, broken up

In a large bowl, beat together your cream cheese and powdered sugar until creamy. Add in your heavy cream and lemon extract, and beat for about 5 minutes until thickened. Fold in the blueberry pie filling, lemon zest (if using) and graham cracker crust pieces until combined.

Cover and refrigerate for at least 3 hours until thickened.

SWEET POTATO PIE FRIES

Sometimes a whole pie is just too much for me. So why not turn them into
little individual servings? Pie fries are exactly what you need. Sweet potato filling
is stuffed between two pie crusts and baked up until golden brown. Cut them into strips
and you can snack on these babies any time the craving hits.

SERVES 6 TO 8

2 (9-inch [23-cm]) refrigerated
pie crusts

1 cup (230 g) cooked and mashed
sweet potatoes

¼ cup (45 g) brown sugar

¼ cup (50 g) plus 1 tbsp (13 g)
granulated sugar, divided

½ tsp cinnamon

¼ tsp nutmeg

¼ tsp salt

1 egg, beaten

Preheat the oven to 350°F (177°C, or gas mark 4). Unroll your pie
crusts and place one on a greased cookie sheet or 10-inch (25-cm)
round pizza pan. Set aside.

In a medium bowl, mix together your mashed sweet potatoes, brown
sugar, ¼ cup (50 g) of granulated sugar, cinnamon, nutmeg and salt.
Spread evenly over the crust, leaving about a ½-inch (13-mm) rim of
crust on all edges. Top with the remaining pie crust, and pinch the sides
together gently.

Brush the beaten egg over the top of the pie crust, and sprinkle with
1 tablespoon (13 g) of sugar. Bake in the oven for 15 to 20 minutes until
slightly golden. Remove from the oven, and let cool for 10 minutes.

Using a knife or pizza cutter, cut down the center and then in 1-inch
(2.5-cm) sections to create fries or sticks.

LEMONADE PUPPY CHOW

Is it Puppy Chow or Muddy Buddies? Where I'm from we grew up saying Puppy Chow. The normal classic chocolate and peanut butter snack takes a twist here with the addition of lemon. Mixing it with white chocolate makes this a seriously addicting treat.

SERVES 6 TO 8

6 cups (186 g) rice cereal such as Chex

2 (4-oz [113-g]) white chocolate baking bars

1 tbsp (15 g) lemon zest

2 tbsp (30 ml) lemon juice

3 tbsp (45 g) unsalted butter

1½ cups (150 g) powdered sugar

Place your cereal in a large bowl. Set aside.

In a medium microwave-safe bowl, add your white chocolate, lemon zest, lemon juice and butter. Microwave in 30-second increments until melted, stirring often. When melted, pour the mixture over your cereal and gently stir to coat.

Add your coated mixture to a large paper bag, then pour your powdered sugar over the top. Roll the top of the bag down to seal, shake gently to coat all the cereal then pour it into a serving bowl.

GINGERBREAD TRUFFLES

When Christmastime rolls around, gingerbread cookies are one of the cookies we never leave out. These Gingerbread Truffles are cookies taken to the next step. Mixed with cream cheese and dipped in almond bark, they are a fun twist on a classic cookie.

MAKES 24

1 (16-oz [450-g]) box gingersnap cookies

1 (8-oz [230-g]) package cream cheese, softened

½ block white chocolate almond bark, melted

Cinnamon, for garnish

In a food processor, add your gingersnap cookies. Process until crumbs form. Add in your cream cheese, and process until combined and blended.

Line a baking sheet with parchment paper. Grab your cookie mixture and roll it into 1- to 2-inch (2.5- to 5-cm) balls. Place them on a baking sheet, then freeze them for 30 minutes.

Remove from the freezer and, using a fork, dunk your truffles one by one in melted almond bark until covered. Place the truffles back on parchment paper, and immediately sprinkle with cinnamon. Let set for 10 minutes before serving.

ITALIAN CREAM COOKIE SALAD

Cookie salad is one of our favorite potluck treats! Pair it with one of my favorite cakes of all time and you have yourself a light and airy dessert filled with coconut, pecans and shortbread. This is one of those desserts that will not have any leftovers at the end of the day.

SERVES 6 TO 8

2 (3.4-oz [96-g]) packages French vanilla pudding

2 cups (475 ml) buttermilk

3 (8-oz [226-g]) containers whipped topping

1½ cups (115 g) shredded sweetened coconut

1 cup (120 g) chopped pecans

1 (16-oz [450-g]) package shortbread cookies, broken up

In a large bowl, mix together your pudding and milk until thickened. Fold in your whipped topping. Fold in your coconut, pecans and your cookies.

Place in the refrigerator to chill for 1 hour before serving.

PUPPY CHOW POPCORN

I've been a longtime extra-buttery popcorn fan, but how about some Puppy Chow Popcorn? This popped treat gets coated with chocolate, peanut butter and powdered sugar—making each handful better than the last.

SERVES 8 TO 10

1 cup (175 g) milk chocolate chips

1 cup (250 g) creamy peanut butter

2 (3-oz [84-g]) bags popcorn, popped

4 cups (400 g) powdered sugar

In a microwave-safe bowl, add your chocolate chips and peanut butter. Microwave in 30-second intervals, stirring each time, until melted.

Place half your popcorn in a large bowl, and drizzle with half your chocolate peanut butter mixture. Add the remaining popcorn, and drizzle with the remaining chocolate peanut butter mixture. Gently stir your popcorn until each piece is coated. Add your popcorn mixture to a large paper bag, and sprinkle with powdered sugar. Seal the bag, and shake for 1 to 2 minutes to coat. Pour into a large bowl, and serve immediately.

BROWNIE PEANUT BUTTER COBBLER

We love brownies, we love peanut butter and we love cobbler. It was only right that we combine the three into one. This chewy, gooey and peanut buttery treat is so rich and addicting, and it's perfect when served with a scoop of ice cream.

SERVES 4 TO 6

BASE

¾ cup (150 g) granulated sugar

1 cup (120 g) all-purpose flour

⅓ cup (35 g) unsweetened cocoa powder

2 tsp (10 g) baking powder

1 tsp salt

½ cup (120 ml) milk

⅓ cup (80 ml) unsalted butter, melted

SWIRL

¼ cup (80 g) unsalted butter, melted

½ cup (50 g) powdered sugar

¾ cup (135 g) creamy peanut butter

½ tsp salt

½ tsp vanilla extract

TOPPING

½ cup (90 g) brown sugar

½ cup (100 g) granulated sugar

¼ cup (25 g) unsweetened cocoa powder

¼ tsp salt

1½ tsp (8 ml) vanilla extract

1¼ cups (300 ml) boiling water

Preheat the oven to 350°F (177°C, or gas mark 4). Spray a 9 x 9–inch (23 x 23–cm) baking dish with nonstick cooking spray. Set aside.

In a bowl, whisk together the sugar, flour, cocoa, baking powder and salt. Set aside.

In another bowl, whisk together the milk and butter. Slowly pour it into the flour mixture, and whisk until combined. Spread into the prepared baking dish. Set aside.

To make the swirl, in another bowl, whisk together the butter, powdered sugar, peanut butter, salt and vanilla. Drizzle the mixture over the base, and swirl around with a knife until combined. Set aside.

To make the topping, in another bowl, whisk together the brown sugar, granulated sugar, cocoa powder and salt. Sprinkle it over the base.

Add the vanilla to the boiling water and slowly pour over the top of your cobbler. Bake in the oven for 40 minutes until just barely set in the center. Cool for 10 minutes before serving.

COTTON CANDY ICE CREAM

Raise your hand if you're a cotton candy lover! Who doesn't enjoy a little (or a lot!) of this favorite carnival treat? Well let's give it a makeover and turn it into ice cream! You get the fluffy treat flavor in each and every bite of this frozen favorite.

SERVES 8

2 cups (480 ml) heavy whipping cream

1 (14-oz [396-g]) can sweetened condensed milk

2 tsp (10 ml) cotton candy flavoring

Blue food coloring

Pink food coloring

In a stand mixer fitted with the whisk attachment, add your heavy cream. Whisk until stiff peaks form. Fold in your sweetened condensed milk and cotton candy flavoring.

Separate your mixture into two bowls, and add a few drops of blue food coloring to one bowl and a few drops of pink food coloring to the other bowl. Stir until the color is absorbed.

In a 9 x 5-inch (23 x 13-cm) bread pan, spread your pink mixture, then spoon your blue mixture over the top and spread it out gently. Cover with tinfoil, and freeze for 6 to 8 hours before serving.

ACKNOWLEDGMENTS

First and foremost, I want to thank my entire family for being a part of this journey with me, for putting up with me and a busy schedule, always being around to taste test, lending an ear to ideas and generally just being an amazing support system.

To the publisher, for seeing something in me and thinking that I had enough value to create *Untraditional Desserts* and for putting up with me asking numerous questions and letting me go on the path I wanted to see for this book.

To my husband's and mother's coworkers, for lovingly taking leftovers and always giving me constructive feedback—whether it was good or bad, it was always helpful.

To my friend Susanne, for being there from dusk till dawn, always checking up on me and my progress, helping me with ideas and listening to me whine when something didn't go my way. You were always patient and kind, and I thank you for that.

To my blogging friends, thank you for being people I can talk to about food to no end, knowing what this life is like and always getting me when other people didn't.

To my mom, for inspiring me to cook and bake and hone my creativity. Even though she is the pickiest of eaters, she still loved hearing and seeing what I was able to come up with.

To my husband, who loathed sweets to start with, but now has come around—all thanks to me, so in reality he should be thanking me for opening his eyes to the sweeter things in life.

To my readers, thank you from the bottom of my heart for your loyalty, your support, your comments and your interactions with me. Without you, I would never be where I am today. Without all of you cooking and baking and sharing in my journey, I wouldn't have ever been able to be who I am.

To anyone who has ever had an impact in my life to inspire, encourage and guide me on a journey that has had its ups and downs, I thank you for being part of my life no matter how big or small it has been.

ABOUT THE AUTHOR

Allison Miller is the creator of the popular website Tornadough Alli. Tornadough Alli was created in 2015 and is viewed by millions of people each and every year.

Allison, or Alli, is a writer, photographer, recipe developer and video creator. She lives in west central Minnesota with her husband, Jeremy, their three sons, Jaiden, Keagen and Avery and their daughter, Novalee, along with their fur-babies Phoebe and Thora.

A self-taught cook, she has navigated the kitchen her entire life honing her skills and finding out what works together and what doesn't. She doesn't shy away when it comes to flavor, and she constantly pushes the bar.

She's held many jobs over the years, but she always comes back to baking and cooking as her true passion—when you can do what you love every single day of your life you can hardly call that a job.

When she's not working she enjoys traveling, binge watching Netflix, shopping (duh) and long romantic walks to the fridge. She aspires to keep on writing and creating more recipes that everyone can enjoy and fall in love with as much as she has.

She has been featured on MSN, Buzzfeed, *Country Living*, *Good Housekeeping*, *Parade* and *Better Homes & Gardens*.

INDEX